SPACE INNOVATIONS

# SATELLITES

Ron Miller

Twenty-First Century Books
Minneapolis

To Judith, as faithful a satellite as anyone could wish

Twenty-First Century Books
A division of Lerner Publishing Group, Inc.
241 First Avenue North
Minneapolis, MN 55401 U.S.A.

Website address: www.lernerbooks.com

Library of Congress Cataloging in Publication Data

Miller, Ron, 1947–
Satellites / by Ron Miller.
p. cm. — (Space innovations)
Includes bibliographical references and index.
ISBN-13: 978–0–8225–7154–4 (lib. bdg. : alk. paper)
1. Artificial satellites—History—Juvenile literature. I. Title. II. Series.
TL793.3.M55 2008
629.44 dc22 2007001075

Manufactured in the United States of America
1 2 3 4 5 6 – DP – 13 12 11 10 09 08

# CONTENTS

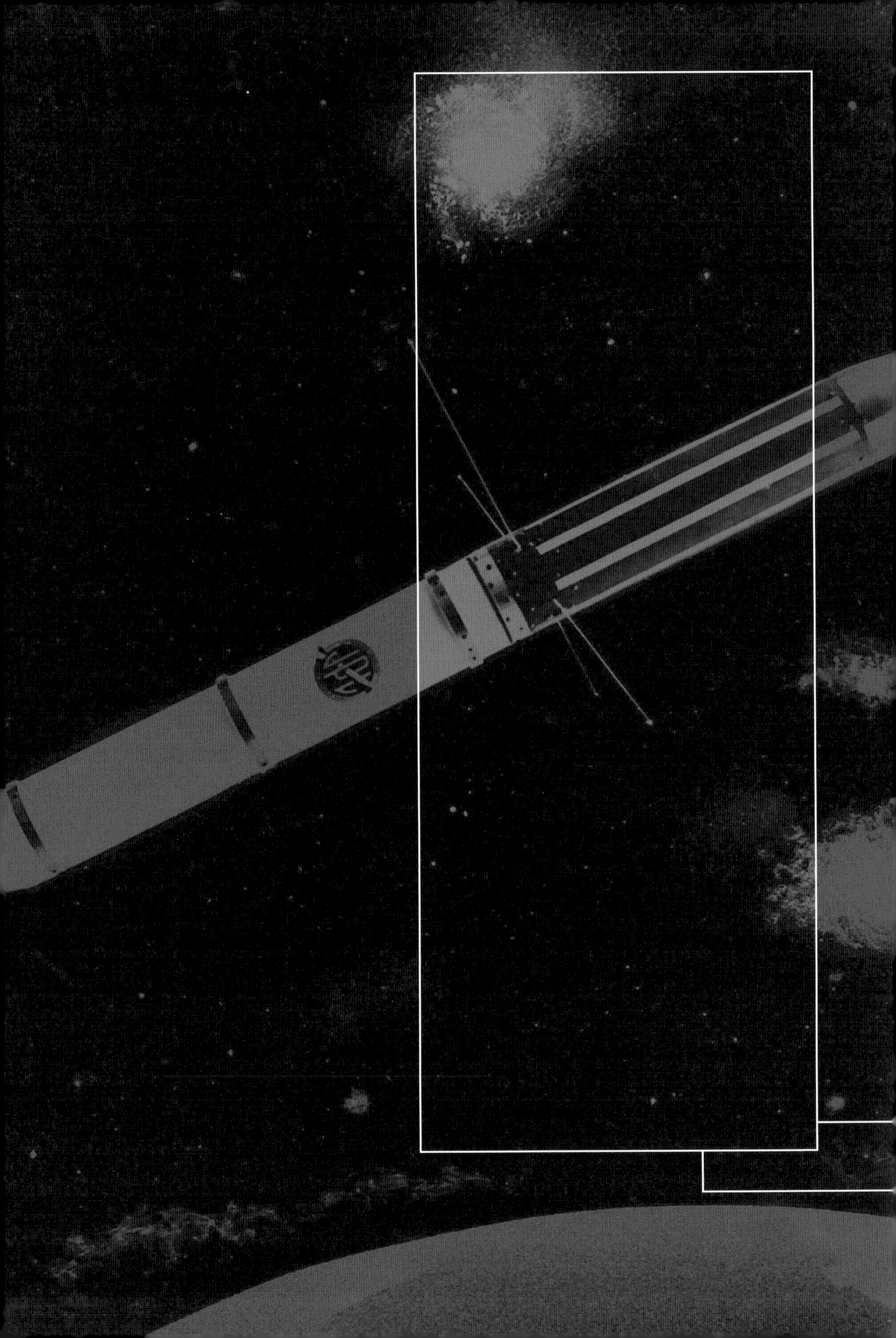

# INTRODUCTION

Once upon a time, Earth had only one companion, the Moon. Nowadays, thousands of new companions circle our planet. Most of them are invisible, but on a dark, clear night, you might be able to spot one or more small dots of light drifting slowly through the sky. They are among the many new companions, or satellites, Earth has gained in the past fifty years. These new satellites are called artificial satellites to distinguish them from the Moon, Earth's natural satellite.

The word *satellite* means "companion." In many ways, these new companions are as remarkable as the original one. You can watch television shows and movies beamed from satellites orbiting more than 12,000 miles (19,312 kilometers) overhead. You can call almost anyone on Earth via signals bounced from other satellites. You know what the weather will be next week because of the instruments aboard weather satellites. You enjoy the benefits of oil and mineral deposits discovered by orbiting sensors. Food at your local market is better because satellites keep a close watch on crops.

Some satellites enable you to pinpoint your location to within a few feet anywhere on the planet. This is done by using a small, inexpensive Global Positioning System (GPS) receiver. The same receiver buried within the electronics of a car allows drivers to view maps of their routes.

Although the first satellite was not launched until fifty years ago, their many uses have made satellites one of the most important inventions ever. Yet as modern as satellites are, their history goes back nearly four hundred years.

(*Facing page*) An artist's depiction of the *Explorer 1* satellite orbiting Earth

# Cannonballs and Brick Moons

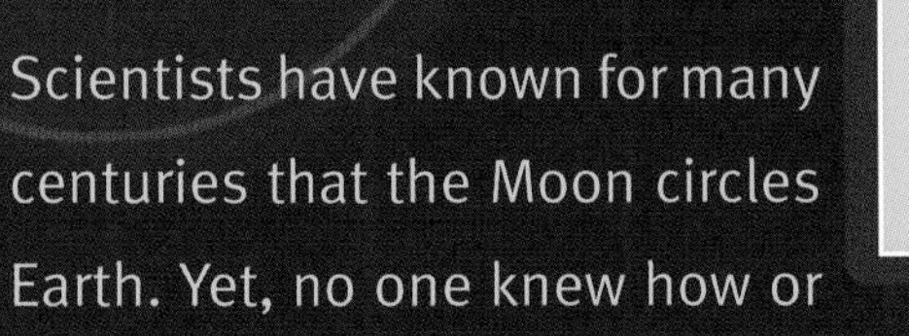

# 1

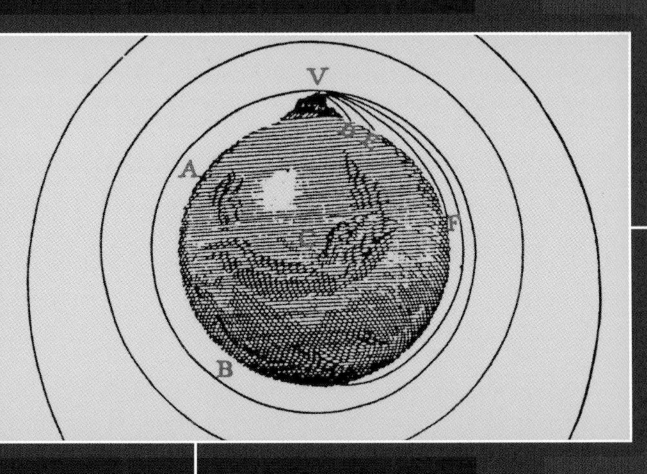

*Top:* Isaac Newton's diagram illustrating how an object could orbit Earth. *Middle:* Edward Everett Hale, author of *The Brick Moon* (1869), which described the first fictional Earth satellite. *Bottom:* An artist's depiction of Hale's Brick Moon

Scientists have known for many centuries that the Moon circles Earth. Yet, no one knew how or why until Sir Isaac Newton (1642–1727), the great English mathematician and scientist, put his powerful brain to work on the subject. Like everyone else, Newton knew that anything unsupported will fall to the ground. As the saying goes, "What goes up must come down."

Legend has it that while watching an apple fall from a tree, Newton asked *why*? If what goes up must come down, then why doesn't the Moon fall to Earth? What keeps it up in the sky? Newton published his answer in his three-volume book *Philosophiae Naturalis Principia Mathematica* (1687)—usually called the *Principia*.

If it were not for the force of gravity, Newton wrote in the *Principia*, a projectile, such as one fired from a cannon, would not fall toward Earth. It would go off from Earth in a straight line. Gravity draws the path of the cannonball into a curve that eventually meets the surface of Earth. If a cannonball, he said, were shot from the top of a mountain, it might travel 2 miles (3.2 km) before its curved path caused it to hit the ground. If the power of the cannon is increased, the cannonball will fly farther.

In this illustration from the original edition of *Principia*, Newton shows how a satellite could be made to circle Earth forever. He imagined a mountain (V) so tall that its peak was above Earth's atmosphere. On the peak was a powerful cannon. If it fired cannonballs with increasingly large amounts of gunpowder, they might fall first to D, then E, and then F. Each time, Earth's gravity would pull the cannonball back to the ground—but each time the curve of the cannonball's path became longer. Eventually, Newton pointed out, the curve of the cannonball's path (A) would match that of Earth beneath it (B). When this happens, the cannonball will circle Earth forever, always falling toward the ground but never reaching it.

## Isaac Newton

Sir Isaac Newton was an English physicist, mathematician, astronomer, alchemist, and philosopher. Many historians and scientists consider him to be one of the greatest scientists who ever lived. He was the cocreator, along with Gottfried Liebnitz, of the math method called calculus.

In Newton's book *Philosophiae Naturalis Principia Mathematica*, published in 1687, he described the laws by which gravitation affects everything from apples to planets. He also presented three basic laws of motion. He was the first to show that the motion of objects on Earth and the motion of the planets and moons are all governed by the same set of natural laws. These laws helped lay the groundwork for modern rocketry and space exploration.

In addition to his theoretical work in physics and mathematics, Newton was also an inventor and practical experimenter. He created the reflecting telescope. He discovered that white light is actually a combination of the spectrum of colors observed when light passes through a prism. He studied the speed of sound, the nature of light, and proposed a theory on the origin of stars.

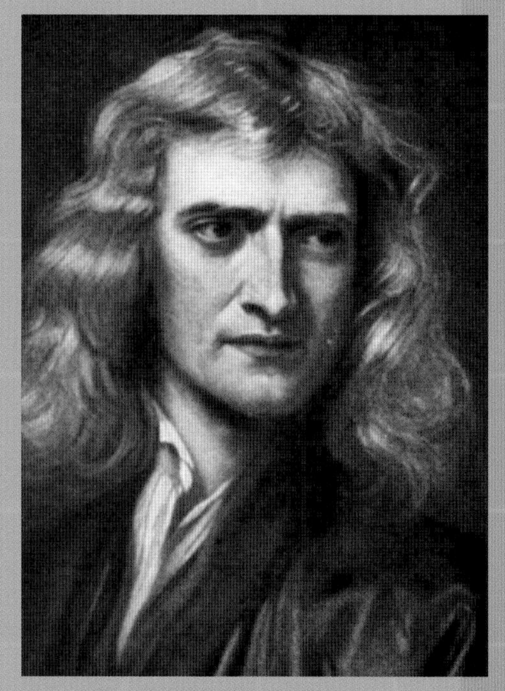

Isaac Newton (1642–1727) was the great English physicist and mathematician who developed the three laws of motion that make rockets and satellites possible.

If the cannon were powerful enough, the curved path of the projectile would be the same as the curvature of the world beneath it. In other words, the cannonball would fall to Earth, but as it approached the ground, the ground would curve away from underneath it. It would never hit the ground but would instead keep circling the world forever.

There are three conditions that must be met for this to happen. First, the projectile must be going fast enough. If going too slow, it will fall to the ground. But if it is going too fast, it will shoot away from Earth forever. Second, there must be no air resistance. Friction with the air would slow the projectile. As soon as it started to slow, it would fall. It must therefore orbit above the atmosphere in airless space. And third, the projectile must be launched parallel to the surface of Earth.

Newton had answered the question: why doesn't the Moon fall to Earth? Because, he said, the Moon is going at just the right speed. The closer to Earth an object orbits, the faster it must go in order to balance the pull of Earth's gravity. An object orbiting Earth at a distance of only a few hundred miles has to travel at a speed of several miles a second—orbiting Earth every couple of minutes—in order to stay up. At the distance the Moon orbits, about 240,000 miles (386,000 km), the speed can be a relatively leisurely 0.7 miles a second (1 km/sec). But more important, Newton's explanation for what kept Earth's natural satellite in the sky set the stage for the invention of the artificial satellite.

All of this was interesting to mathematicians and astronomers, but it had no practical value. No cannon was powerful enough to launch a projectile that fast. Plus, it would have had to be launched atop a mountain more than 100 miles (160 km) high! The highest mountain on Earth, Mount Everest, is only 5.5 miles (8.8 km) high. So at that time, no conceivable way existed for such a cannon to be built.

## The Brick Moon

By the middle of the nineteenth century, at least one person began to consider the advantages of placing an artificial moon in the sky. Edward Everett Hale (1822–1909) was a Boston clergyman, writer,

Edward Everett Hale, the author of *The Brick Moon*, was a grandnephew of the Revolutionary War patriot Nathan Hale.

editor, and grandnephew of the Revolutionary War (1775–1783) patriot Nathan Hale. Edward Everett Hale is most famous for his classic short story, "The Man without a Country."

Less famous but perhaps more important was Hale's novel, *The Brick Moon*, which was published in 1869. In it, Hale was the first person since Newton to discuss the possibility of an artificial satellite. Although Newton's satellite was merely an abstract mathematical concept, Hale thought about the practical uses of such a satellite.

The satellite Hale described was to be a huge brick sphere, 200 feet (60 meters) in diameter. Brick was chosen because it could resist the heat of atmospheric friction during launch. Atmospheric friction is a challenge to modern-day rocket and spacecraft designers. As an object travels through the atmosphere, the air passing over it rubs against the surface. This creates heat. The faster the object travels, the more heat is produced. At the great speeds that rockets travel, this can create enough heat to melt the spacecraft. Therefore, heat-resistant materials must be used.

The Brick Moon would be made hollow to keep its weight down. It would be painted white, to make it more visible from Earth's surface. High visibility was necessary to fulfill the main function of the Brick Moon: to act as a navigational aid. In Hale's novel, three moons are planned, so that at least one would always be visible above

In Hale's novel, the inhabitants of the Brick Moon could communicate with Earth by spelling out messages in huge letters on the surface of the satellite. People on Earth could reply the same way.

Earth's horizon. At any given time, navigators on board ships would know exactly how far above Earth a Brick Moon was and what its position should be. Navigators would then be able to calculate the location of their ships with great precision.

Hale had no idea how such a huge object could be launched into orbit. So he invented a method that he hoped would sound possible to his readers—even if it could not work in real life. In the story, the moons are to be flung into orbit as though from a slingshot. This would be done by rolling each of the moons onto a pair of huge, rapidly spinning flywheels.

# Air Friction

Rub the palms of your hands briskly against each other. They will quickly feel warm. This is exactly the same thing that occurs when a rocket passes through Earth's atmosphere. At the thousands of miles an hour a rocket can travel, the friction of air on its surface could cause it to burn up like a meteor. An example of this occurred in February 2003 when the space shuttle *Columbia* disintegrated after reentry. One way to reduce air friction is to construct spacecraft from heat-resistant materials. One problem with this is that once the outside skin of the spacecraft becomes hot, the heat has nowhere to go but inside. This is dangerous for sensitive instruments and for human passengers. The solution was to develop materials that would disintegrate as air friction heated them. As tiny pieces of the material flaked off, they would carry heat with them, keeping it from penetrating the spacecraft. This technique is called ablation.

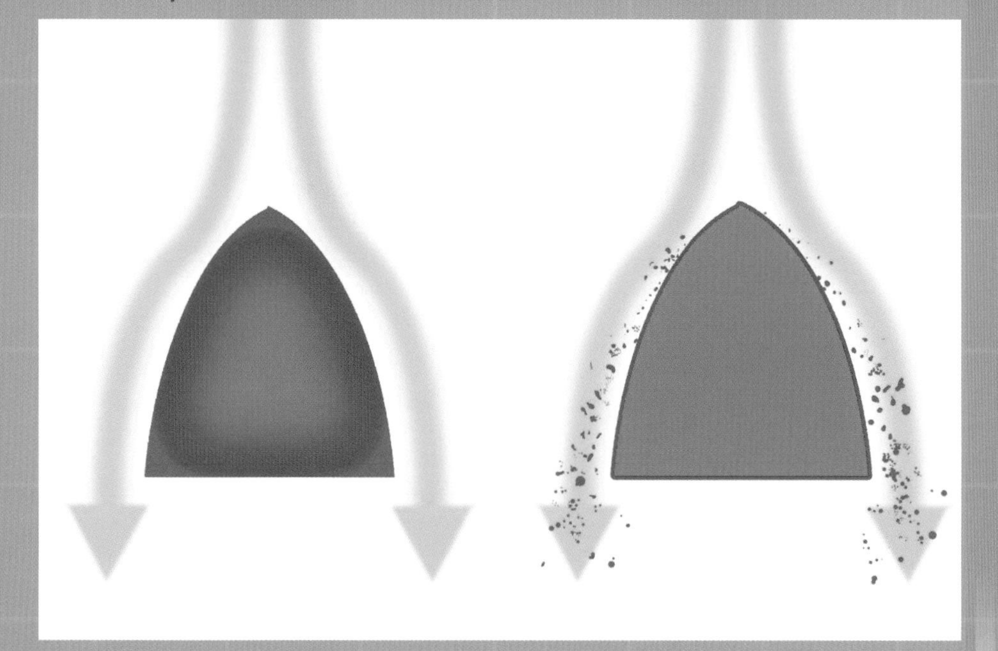

The process of ablation protects an object from intense heat by carrying the heat away safely. As air rushes past the nose cone on the left, friction causes the nose cone to heat up. If this continues, the nose cone may melt. The nose cone on the right, however, has an ablative coating. As this coating heats up, it flakes off, carrying away the excess heat with it.

The first of the moons to be built is accidentally launched early, with the workers and their families still on board. It goes into orbit 5,000 miles (8,000 km) above Earth. The accidental astronauts discover a way to communicate with their friends on Earth. Their observations foreshadow many of the uses of modern-day satellites. They report on weather conditions, for instance, and make geographical and geological observations for scientists on Earth.

Although Hale predicted many of the advantages of an Earth satellite, his story did not cause a stir among the public. It certainly didn't inspire anyone to start thinking about launching a real satellite. This was in large part because of the same problem Hale faced in writing the story: there was no imaginable way to get a satellite of any size—let alone a 200-foot (61 m) brick ball—into space.

Although rockets existed at the time Hale wrote his novel, they were underpowered and unreliable. Even Jules Verne, in his classic science-fiction novel *From the Earth to the Moon* (1865), used a giant cannon instead of a rocket to launch his spaceship. Verne knew that rockets would work in space, but he thought his readers would never believe in a rocket big enough to launch something to the Moon.

# 2 THE ROCKET

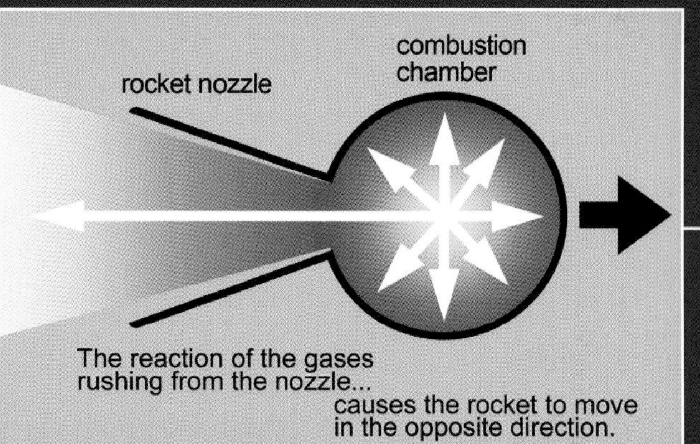


In spite of the poor performance of rockets in the nineteenth century, a few writers and scientists knew that rockets offered the only possibility for leaving Earth. This is because rockets operate on Newton's third law of motion. This law says that for every action, there is an equal but opposite reaction. Rockets fly because the action of the exhaust shooting from one end causes the rocket to move in the opposite direction—an equal but opposite reaction. This means that rockets can fly whether they are operating in an atmosphere like Earth's or in an airless region like outer space.

This is an important distinction when considering alternative forms of flight. Balloons were the only way of leaving the ground during the nineteenth century. But, in order to rise, they required the buoyancy of the atmosphere. They were incapable of rising into the empty space above the atmosphere. Aircraft, which came into successful use at the beginning of the twentieth century, could fly higher than most balloons. But they were still limited to staying within the atmosphere, since their engines needed air. Their wings also needed air to create lift. Rockets were the only answer.

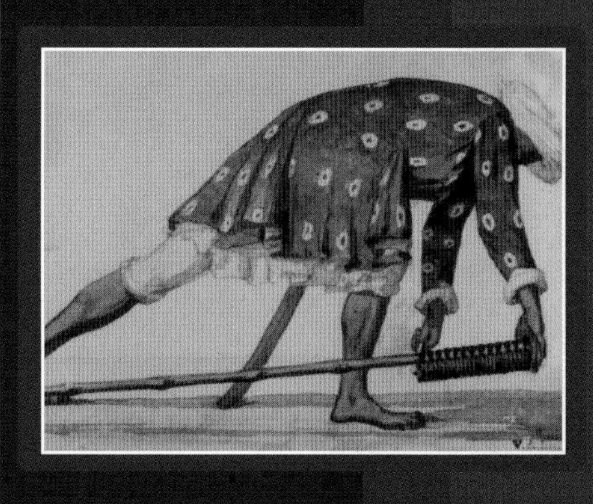

*Top:* This illustration depicts the way rocket propulsion works. *Middle:* An Indian rocketeer prepares a military rocket for launching. *Bottom:* The British used rockets against Americans in the War of 1812 (1812–1815).

The battle at Kai-fung-fu in 1232 is depicted in this 1951 watercolor by artist-historian Jack Coggins.

## Early Rockets

The idea of artificial satellites is relatively new. Newton laid the groundwork a little more than three hundred years ago, but no one seriously considered the possibility until Hale wrote *The Brick Moon* 150 years later. Rockets, however, are an ancient invention.

Rockets were first developed in China, although it's unknown exactly when. One of the earliest references to rockets in Chinese literature is in a book called *Ching Shih* (*History of the Ching Dynasty*), which was written in the fourteenth century. It describes the use of rockets during the siege of the city of Kai-fung-fu in 1232.

# How Rockets Work

The third of Newton's three laws of motion describes how rockets work. It states that for every action there is an equal but opposite reaction. When a gun is fired, the burning gunpowder forces a bullet forward from the barrel. At the same time, the gun moves backward, or in the opposite direction. The opposite movement is called recoil. This raises a question, however. If the opposite reaction is supposed to be equal, why doesn't the gun fly backward with the same force and speed as the bullet? The answer to this lies in Newton's second law of motion. This states that the more massive an object, the slower it is to accelerate. In other words, it is harder to get a heavy object to move than a light one. Since the gun weighs many times more than the bullet, it reacts much less to the force.

If a gun shot out a continuous stream of bullets—like a machine gun—the recoil would be continuous. This is what happens in rockets. The gas molecules produced by the burning fuel act like trillions of tiny, individual bullets. As each one is ejected from the rear of the rocket, the rocket itself is moved in the opposite direction according to Newton's third law.

A rocket does not fly because the exhaust is pushing against the air behind it. In fact, a rocket works better in a vacuum—a space without air or gas—than it does in an atmosphere. In an atmosphere, the air actually gets in the way of the gases being released, which slows down the gases. And the slower the gases travel, the slower the rocket goes.

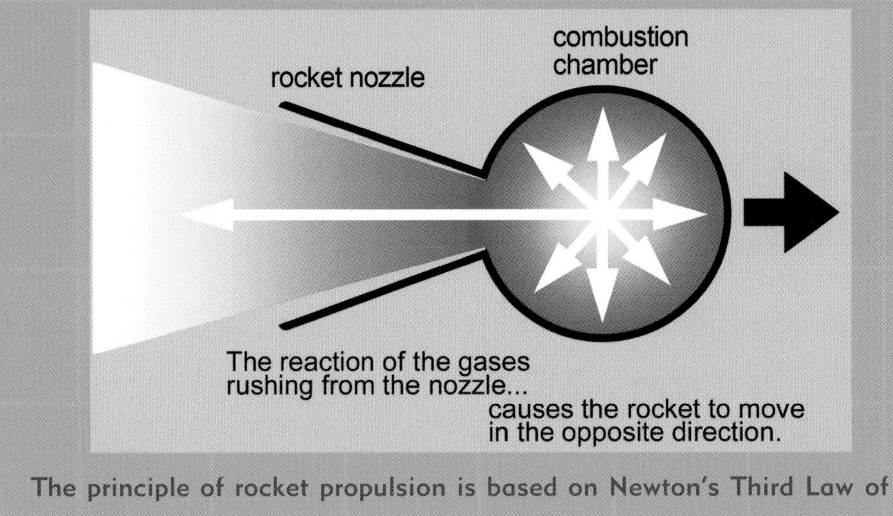


The principle of rocket propulsion is based on Newton's Third Law of Motion: for every action, there is an equal but opposite reaction.

The city was under siege by Mongols, who were unpleasantly surprised by a new weapon they had never before experienced. It was called fe-ee-ho-tsiang, or arrow of flying fire. These rockets carried warheads containing a flammable substance that would explode over a wide area on impact. The rocket itself must have been invented much earlier, however, for such an advanced version to be available at that date and for the Chinese soldiers to be so adept in its use.

No one knows exactly what the first rockets looked like. They were probably ordinary arrows with rockets attached, since pictures of later rockets were shown to look like this. Even as late as 1900, Chinese fireworks rockets often had feathers attached to the ends of their sticks. This was a carryover from their ancient origins as fire arrows (and a useless one too, since the exhaust of the rocket probably quickly burned away the feathers).

Early rockets could not be aimed with much accuracy. Once they were launched, they pretty much went where they pleased. But by launching hundreds at the same time, the Chinese were assured of the rockets having at least some effect on their enemies. The sight and sound of masses of flaming rockets arching through the air and exploding everywhere must have been terrifying to the enemy.

It did not take long for the secret of the new weapon to leak out. In a book written around 1249, the English monk Roger Bacon included instructions for making gunpowder and rockets, though he used a code that kept many people from learning those secrets.

Rockets were quickly adapted by the military of many countries. They were used in warfare as early as 1258. Rockets were used successfully in the battle for the Isle of Chiozza in Italy in 1379. One historian's discussion of the siege described the new weapon as a *rocchetto*. This is the Italian word for a small spindle, which rockets resembled. It is also the word from which the modern English word *rocket* is derived.

# The Rise of the Rocket

For more than six hundred years, rocket enthusiasts in many European countries tried to persuade the military to use rockets as weapons. The armies of a few countries set up rocket battalions. Some of these battalions performed well in combat. But by the first decades of the seventeenth century, the use of rockets by the military became less frequent.

This was mainly because rockets were unreliable. Once a rocket has taken off, there is no guarantee that it will go where it's supposed to. In order for even a few rockets to hit their target, dozens and perhaps even hundreds had to be launched. Rockets were therefore relegated to playing a relatively small role—mostly in entertaining fireworks displays. (This was not the case at sea, however. Sailors used rockets for sending signals, and pirates used them to set fire to other ships.)

It eventually took an embarrassing military defeat to convince the British military of the value of rockets. At the end of the eighteenth century, Great Britain's efforts to colonize India were well under way. The native Indians resisted the invading British forces. In at least one battle, this resistance took an entirely unexpected form.

Prince Hydar Ali of Mysore was one of the Indian rulers who most actively resisted the British invasion. In addition to his regular army, the prince formed a company of 1,200 rocket gunners. The rockets these men launched at their enemy were not the cardboard rockets the British were accustomed to seeing at royal fireworks displays. They were iron tubes weighing 6 to 12 pounds (2.7 to 5.4 kilograms), guided by 10-foot (3 m) bamboo sticks.

These rockets could carry a warhead made from the end of a sword or a sharpened stake anywhere from 1 to 1.5 miles (1.6 to 2.4 km). They were not too accurate, but when hundreds were launched at the same time, accuracy didn't matter. At least *one* rocket would hit *something*. The British suffered severe defeats in 1792 and 1799 due

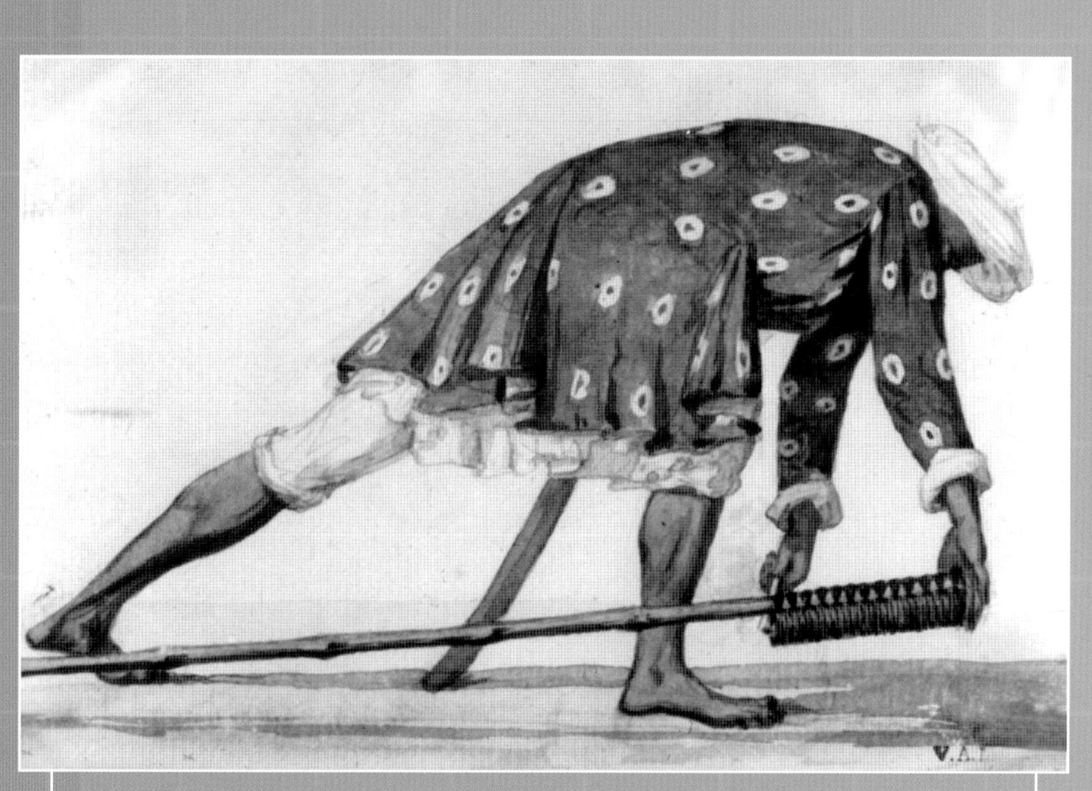

An Indian rocketeer prepares to launch his rocket. The effect of rockets such as this one impressed William Congreve a great deal.

to the effective use of rockets by the Indian armies. The British army began to reconsider its low opinion of the rocket's value as a weapon.

Colonel William Congreve immediately purchased the largest skyrockets he could find in London, paying for them himself. He began a series of tests to see just how far an existing British rocket could travel. This turned out to be about 600 yards (550 m), only half the distance of an Indian war rocket. He took this information to the Royal Laboratory at Woolwich and obtained permission to use the laboratory and its firing ranges.

With the use of these facilities, Congreve soon developed a rocket capable of flying 2,000 yards (1,830 m). The government quickly approved the use of rockets by the navy. The navy used them to devastating effect in attacks against Boulogne, France, and Copenhagen, Denmark. Most of Copenhagen was burned to the

During the War of 1812, British rocket boats fired on Maryland's Fort McHenry in Baltimore Harbor. The rocketeers wore heavy leather coats to protect them from the fiery exhaust of their missiles. This event, which is memorialized in the words "the rockets' red glare" in the U.S. national anthem, was depicted in 1951 in this watercolor by artist-historian Jack Coggins.

ground after a barrage consisting of hundreds of rockets.

Congreve was convinced that his rockets would soon replace artillery on the battlefield. They were inexpensive to manufacture and relatively easy to use. They were light and easily movable and neither more nor less accurate than the artillery of the time. Eventually, the British adopted Congreve's rockets and used them successfully in many battles. "The rockets' red glare" is mentioned in the U.S. national anthem. It refers to the British rockets that were fired at Fort McHenry in Baltimore, Maryland, during the War of 1812.

## The Fall of the Rocket

Rockets had proved effective in battle time and again. They were eventually adapted by many other countries, which formed their own rocket troops. But the rocket still had its faults. The long, cumbersome guide stick was a big problem.

The purpose of the guide stick was to help balance the rocket, enabling it to fly straighter than it would on its own. But guide sticks were only partially effective. The entire rocket would start off balance at launch, but as its fuel was used up, its weight would change. The weight of the stick, however, never changed. So the balance of the entire rocket would eventually be thrown off, and it would veer off course. The long guide sticks also made the rockets difficult to transport.

A number of inventors tried to do away with the guide stick and stabilize the rocket in some other way. They had high hopes but unsatisfactory results. A British inventor named William Hale (no known relation to Nathan or Edward Everett Hale) finally solved the problem in 1844 by getting rid of the guide stick entirely. To stabilize his rockets, Hale inserted three curved metal vanes in the exhaust nozzle. These vanes caused the rocket to spin rapidly when launched.

Making a projectile spin had long been recognized as the best way to achieve stability and straight flight. Newton's first law of motion states that once an object is set in motion, it will tend to remain in motion unless acted upon by an outside force. This means that once an object is set spinning, it will resist any change in the direction of that spin. Just as a spinning top will resist being pushed over, a spinning bullet or rocket will resist being turned from its path.

Hale's rockets were a great improvement over the Congreve version. But the invention arrived too late. By then the accuracy and firepower of cannons had far exceeded the capability of the unreliable rocket, which usually had to be fired in large numbers to ensure hitting a target. An entirely new type of rocket was needed, but that had to wait until the dawn of the following century.

# 3

# THE DREAMERS

*Top:* Robert Goddard poses with the first-ever liquid-fuel rocket in 1926. *Middle:* Hermann Oberth laid much of the theoretical groundwork for modern astronautics. *Bottom:* The space station designed by Hermann Potočnik in 1929 was the first serious engineering study for such a project.

Science-fiction authors such as Edward Everett Hale and Jules Verne had described artificial satellites in their stories and novels. But the idea of an Earth-circling satellite was not taken seriously until 1903, when Konstantin E. Tsiolkovsky described one in an article published in a popular Russian science magazine.

Tsiolkovsky, one of the great, formative geniuses in the early history of spaceflight, was born in Russia in 1857. When he was ten, a bout with scarlet fever left him almost completely deaf. This made it difficult for him to attend school, so he studied at home. He read every book he could get his hands on, especially books about mathematics and physics. He did so well that he was offered a job as a teacher at the age of nineteen. He remained a teacher, working at several different schools, for the rest of his career.

Tsiolkovsky never lost interest in science and research, however. Every day, after his teaching duties had been completed, he hurried home to work on his own projects. One of these projects concerned the possibility of exploring outer space.

Konstantin E. Tsiolkovsky (1857–1935), the Russian schoolteacher who helped found modern astronautics

In his 1903 article and later papers, he described how a rocket launched from Earth could become an artificial satellite, circling the planet forever. He explained that it would have to be launched at the proper speed and angle. He went on to describe the kinds of observations its passengers might be able to make, such as tracking Earth's weather or spying on military movements.

About twelve years later, a shy mathematics teacher from Romania named Hermann Oberth independently developed the same idea as Tsiolkovsky. Oberth had long been fascinated by the space travel stories of Jules Verne and Kurd Lasswitz, a German science-fiction writer. Oberth combined his interest in mathematics and physics and started to work on a mathematical theory of space travel. In 1923 he published all of his ideas in a slim little book called *Die Rakete zu den Planetenräumen* (The Rocket into Planetary Space).

In the final chapter of his book, Oberth described an Earth satellite that could carry passengers. "If we let such rockets," he wrote, "move around the Earth in a circle they will behave like a small moon. Such rockets no longer need to be designed for landing.

Hermann Oberth (1894–1985) published his ninety-two-page book on astronautics in 1923 when he was only twenty-eight years old. It became one of the cornerstones of modern spaceflight technology.

Contact between them and the Earth can be maintained by means of smaller rockets so that the large ones (let's call them observing stations) can be rebuilt in the orbit the better to suit their purpose."

Unlike anyone who had thought about Earth satellites before, Oberth described them in detail. He considered the size of the rockets and how they would be launched, how they would be supplied from Earth, and even the effects of weightlessness on the crew. Oberth went on to describe all the possible practical uses for a satellite. One of his ideas was to construct a huge mirror in space. This could be used to provide light in arctic regions during their long winter nights and perhaps even prevent ice from forming in northern shipping lanes.

Oberth's book was enormously influential. It was not mere speculation. It placed the possibility of spaceflight and Earth satellites on a firm, mathematical foundation. The only thing missing was a rocket powerful enough to launch a satellite into space. The old gunpowder rockets of the nineteenth century would never be powerful enough to do the job. An entirely new kind of rocket was needed.

## Solid Fuel vs. Liquid Fuel

All rockets operate the same way. Gas is ejected from one end to make the rocket go forward in accordance with Newton's third law of motion. The faster the gas is ejected, the faster the rocket will go. Scientists needed a way to make the gas go faster than it ever had before.

For several hundred years, rockets burned solid fuel. This solid fuel usually took the form of gunpowder—a mixture of sulfur, charcoal, and potassium nitrate. The sulfur and charcoal provided the fuel. The potassium nitrate provided a source of oxygen that burned the fuel. This mixture was packed into a tube with one open end. When the gunpowder was ignited, it created a jet of hot gas that propelled the rocket forward.

Solid-fuel rockets have a number of advantages. They are extremely simple, powerful, and easy to manufacture and store. However, they cannot be easily controlled. Once a solid-fuel rocket starts to burn, it is virtually impossible to turn it off. And the rate of the burning cannot be controlled, so the rocket cannot be slowed down or sped up.

The invention of the liquid-fuel rocket changed all that. Instead of mixing the oxidizer and fuel into a solid mass, the two remain separate. They are also liquids, which can be easily stored in tanks. For example, most liquid-fuel rockets use liquid oxygen as their oxidizer. Almost anything that burns, such as kerosene or gasoline, can be used as a fuel. Powerful pumps force these liquids into a part of the engine called the combustion chamber, where they mix and are ignited. The speed of the pumps can be controlled or turned off entirely. Therefore, the rocket engine's speed can be controlled and the engine can also be started and stopped at will.

A liquid-fuel rocket is much more complex than a solid-fuel rocket. For example, it requires unique fuel tanks, pumps, and a specific type of

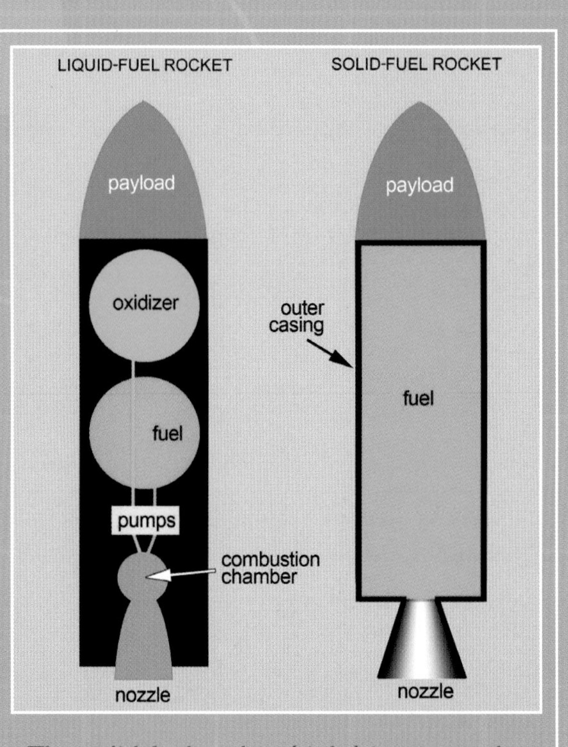


The solid-fuel rocket *(right)* is extremely simple. A cylinder is packed with propellant. When the propellant is burned, the resulting gases shoot from a nozzle at one end of the rocket. Solid-fuel rockets are inexpensive and relatively simple to make, but they have several problems. The first is that solid fuels do not produce as much energy as liquid fuels. A second problem is that once it is started, a solid-fuel rocket cannot be throttled or turned off. A liquid-fuel rocket *(left)* solves these problems—though at the expense of being much more complicated and difficult to build. Because the fuel and oxidizer are kept separate and fed into the motor by pumps or a pressurized gas, the liquid-fuel motor can be easily controlled and even turned off and restarted.

motor. But its advantages far outweigh its disadvantages. This is especially true since liquid fuels are much more powerful—pound for pound—than solid fuels.

The idea of a liquid-fuel rocket had been first proposed at the end of the nineteenth century. But it was not until March 16, 1926, that the first liquid-fuel rocket was launched. After several years of experimentation, physics professor Robert Goddard took his rocket and its launching frame to a snow-covered field on a relative's farm. His wife and two men from the college where he taught accompanied him. The "rocket" Goddard constructed would hardly be recognizable today. It was little more than a fragile-looking framework of thin pipes connecting the fuel and oxidizer tanks to the motor.

Robert Goddard (1882–1945) poses beside his first liquid-fuel rocket shortly before it made its first flight, on March 16, 1926, from a field near Auburn, Massachusetts.

Launching the rocket was simple. The fuel and oxidizer valves were opened while Goddard's assistant held a blowtorch attached to a short pole. He held the flame under the rocket's nozzle. The motor erupted with a shrill roar, and the rocket lifted from its frame. After only two and a half seconds, its fuel was used up. The rocket dropped back to the ground.

It had traveled a distance of 184 feet (56 m) and achieved a speed of about 60 miles (97 km) per hour. This is unimpressive even by the standards of a small gunpowder skyrocket. But still, it was the flight of the world's first liquid-fuel rocket. It was the powerful, reliable liquid-fuel rocket that made the idea of an artificial, Earth-circling satellite possible.

## The Man Who Invented the Space Station

In 1929 another important book in the history of Earth satellites was published. It was written by a captain in the Austro-Hungarian army engineer corps named Hermann Potočnik. Potočnik book, *The Problem of Space Travel*, was published under the pseudonym Hermann Noordung. It describes in detail how a manned space station would be constructed and what it would look like.

Potočnik wheel-shaped station rotated in order to provide the crew with artificial gravity. Its power was generated by solar energy. The station was equipped with air locks to allow space-suited crew members to enter and exit. It even provided an orbiting space telescope for the astronauts. Potočnik was the first person to suggest that radio might be used for communication between the station and Earth.

Although Potočnik book was available only in a German-language edition, it became extremely influential. This is because portions of the book were translated into English and other languages and published in magazines. The illustrations of the space station were widely reproduced. Even people who were unaware of the original source were inspired by the design.

All the artificial Earth satellites that had been envisioned until Potočnik time had required an onboard crew. That is, they were kinds of space stations. This was because no one could then imagine any way in which information (such as photographs of Earth) could be gathered unless it was done by human beings. Nor could anyone envision a practical way in which this information could be transferred to Earth. Potočnik did suggest radio communication, but physical things such as photos would have to be returned by means of rockets. In short, the technology to transmit radio communications from space—or even to build a small, unmanned communication satellite—did not exist.

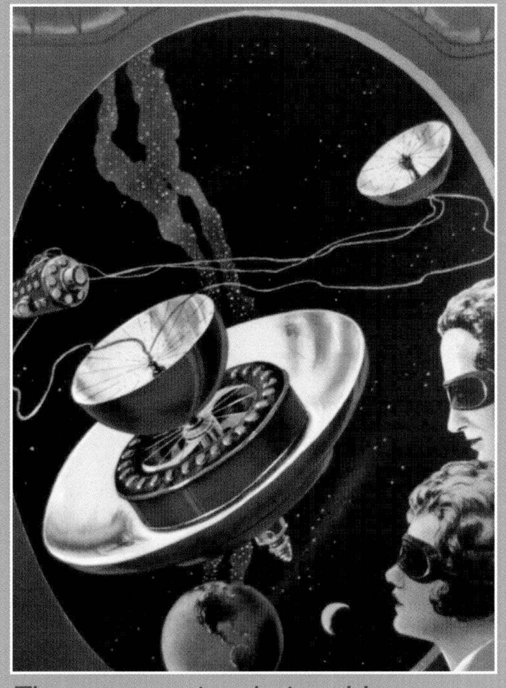

The space station designed by Hermann Potočnik (1892–1929) is depicted in this 1929 painting by Frank R. Paul. It shows the main station in the foreground, a solar power generator at the upper right, and a space telescope on the upper left. Power cables connect all three structures.

Communication was not the only problem that curbed research on artificial satellites. There was still the question of how to get satellites into orbit. It was generally agreed that it would need to be done by rockets. But the biggest rocket anyone was able to build in the 1920s was barely able to lift itself 1,000 feet (305 m) off the ground. It would never be powerful enough to lift a payload into orbit. Until such a rocket was built, all ideas about orbiting satellites were little more than fantasies.

# 4

# BEYOND THE BLUE HORIZON

It's almost impossible to declare precisely where Earth's atmosphere ends and space begins. Earth's atmosphere does not end abruptly, like the surface of the water in an aquarium. Instead, it gradually becomes thinner and thinner until it is scarcely distinguishable from empty space. For all practical purposes, however, scientists usually say space begins about 62 miles (100 km) above Earth's surface (though molecules of Earth's atmosphere may extend as far as 2,000 miles [3,200 km]).

By the end of World War II (1939–1945), the ways to explore the upper regions of Earth's atmosphere were still limited. Aircraft with air-breathing engines could go only as

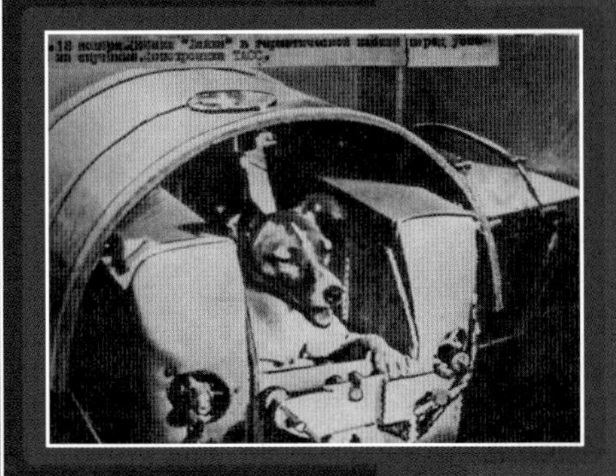

*Top*: A rocket in the Project Bumper series takes off in July 1950. *Middle:* An artist's depiction shows *Vanguard 1* in orbit over Earth. It would have been the United States' first Earth satellite if problems with its booster hadn't delayed its launch until 1957. *Bottom:* Laika, the first living space traveler, sits in her space capsule in 1957.

A stratosphere balloon is launched in 1932. A pair of scientists were carried aloft in a small, sealed aluminum sphere, just barely visible at the bottom of the picture.

high as about 6 miles (8 km). Instrument-carrying balloons could reach nearly 20 miles (32 km). But this was still only a fraction of the distance that separated Earth's surface from outer space. However, both the United States and the Soviet Union (USSR—present-day Russia and its fifteen surrounding republics) soon acquired the means to reach the upper limits of the atmosphere.

## Project Blossom

The giant V-2 rocket had been developed by the Germans in the late 1930s and early 1940s. They developed instruments for the V-2 with which they hoped to study the upper atmosphere. But wartime priorities prevented them from actually doing this. At the end of the war, the United States and the Soviets, who had been allies during the war, captured hundreds of V-2 rockets and rocket parts. They also acquired the scientists and engineers who had developed the missile.

One of the most knowledgeable German scientists brought back to the United States was Wernher von Braun. Von Braun was an outspoken, articulate, and energetic supporter of spaceflight. In addition to his scientific and engineering genius, he had an enthusiasm that quickly infected others. Von Braun had been an important member of a German rocket society that was established before the war. He had been in charge of developing the V-2 rocket.

The United States and the Soviet Union immediately began programs to use the V-2 rockets for scientific research. The German scientists were crucial to the development of both countries' space programs. In fact, when the Soviets finally launched the first Earth satellite, they joked—with a measure of truth—that their Germans had beaten America's Germans.

The United States began launching its reconstructed V-2s at the White Sands Missile Range in New Mexico. The first instrument-carrying rocket was launched on May 10, 1946. It reached an altitude of 70 miles (113 km) and returned information about cosmic rays.

Instruments weren't the only things the U.S. V-2 rockets carried into near space. The Air Force Cambridge Research Laboratory Field Station at White Sands Missile Range started Project Blossom. The U.S. Air Force intended to test methods of recovering payloads from the fringes of space. Ten flights were planned in which V-2 payloads would be recovered by parachute. This included the safe recovery of animals. Canisters containing insects and plants were launched. Even mice and monkeys rode in the missiles. The recovery rate was not always successful.

The first Project Blossom rocket lifted off on February 20, 1947. At its farthest distance from Earth, it ejected its nose cone. An 8-foot (2.4 m) ribbonlike parachute was deployed. As the payload lowered to an altitude of 30 miles (48 km), it deployed another parachute that was 14 feet (4.3 m) in diameter. After falling for fifty minutes, the first Blossom came to rest on the ground. It broke the record for the altitude of a parachute drop.

The experimenters then acquired a larger V-2 rocket and added a bigger payload capsule to it. A monkey named Albert II was a passenger on V-2 No. 47. No fewer than a dozen instruments were on board. The instruments were supposed to gather information about high-energy particles, X-rays, upper atmospheric weather, and air composition.

V-2 No. 47 took off on June 14, 1949. The payload separated from the rocket as planned, but the parachute failed to deploy. The Blossom recovery system continued to fail on later launches. The experimenters finally concluded that parachutes could not be recovered from extremely high altitudes.

## Project Bumper

Project Bumper made an even greater impact than all the previous V-2 flights. During this project, V-2 rockets were launched while carrying a smaller U.S.-designed WAC-Corporal rocket in their noses. When the V-2s reached their maximum speed, the smaller rocket was fired, adding its speed to the speed gained from the larger rocket.

# The First Space Travelers

During and after the 1940s, the U.S. Air Force began sending animals into space. Human space travel depended on whether the animals survived the trip. Insects were among the first animal astronauts. This was mainly because larger, heavier animals would have added weight to the rocket. They also would have required life-support systems.

The first primates sent close to space were two monkeys named Albert I and Albert II. Later V-2 rockets carried Air Force Aero Medical Laboratory monkeys named Albert III and Albert IV. They survived the trip up, but like Albert I and Albert II, they died when their rockets' parachutes failed to open and the nose cones crashed into the ground.

On September 20, 1951, the U.S. Air Force launched an Aerobee rocket that carried a monkey named Yorick and eleven mice. The animals soared to a height of 45 miles (72 km) and returned safely to the ground. It was the first successful round-trip flight of living creatures to the edge of space.

This monkey, named Able, was one of the United States' early space travelers. Here he is seen being prepared for a trip into space aboard an Aerobee rocket in 1959. The lessons learned from this test and others helped prepare for the safe launch and successful return of a human astronaut in 1961.

A rocket in the Project Bumper series is launched in July 1950. When the large V-2 booster reached its maximum speed, the smaller WAC-Corporal in its nose would be fired. Adding its speed to what it had gained from the V-2, the WAC-Corporal could reach record heights.

Only the first of four launches was successful. But when *Bumper 5* was launched in 1949, it reached an altitude of 248 miles (399 km) and a speed of 7,553 feet (2,302 m) per second. This set an altitude and speed record. The little WAC-Corporal had reached outer space.

It was finally possible to send objects beyond Earth's atmosphere. So a number of people started thinking seriously about launching an Earth-circling artificial satellite. As early as 1946, the U.S. Navy considered placing an instrument-carrying satellite into orbit. A year later, the RAND Corporation—a company that conducts research projects for the government—proposed a design for a world-circling spaceship that the air force took very seriously. The navy then had the idea for a High Altitude Test Vehicle. This was supposed to orbit Earth at an altitude of 149 miles (240 km).

The various branches of the U.S. military were finally accepting the idea of an artificial Earth satellite. This turned out to be both a blessing and a curse. Rather than working together on a single design, rivalry between the services made each want to be the first to launch a successful satellite. This led to an embarrassing situation for the United States.

## Getting Closer to Space

Several ideas for artificial satellites were proposed in the early 1950s. Most of these stressed the minimum that could be done with technology of the time, since this would result in the least expensive satellite. And it would be the least expensive and least complicated that would have the best chance to obtain funding. For instance, three members of the British Interplanetary Society—K. W. Gatland, A. M. Kunesch, and A. E. Dixon—suggested a Minimum Satellite Vehicle. One of the proposed versions would have been capable of placing a 485-pound (220 kg) satellite into orbit.

In 1953 Professor S. Fred Singer of the University of Maryland proposed MOUSE: the Minimum Orbital Unmanned Satellite of Earth. Unlike most others who had proposed satellite designs, Singer paid little attention to the rocket. Instead, he concentrated on what the satellite itself would be like. What would it explore? What sort of instruments would it need to carry? In answering these and other questions, Singer developed a spherical shell weighing about 100 pounds (45 kg). This was just about the right size and weight for the job and the rockets that were then available. Singer's ideas were very influential.

# MULTISTAGE ROCKETS

As a rocket travels, its fuel and oxidizer tanks empty. Since the empty tanks are of no use, their extra weight only serves to slow down the rocket. If it were possible to cut away the empty part of the fuel tanks as they drain, the rocket would be lighter and could go higher and faster. This is what happens in a staged rocket. But instead of literally cutting away the empty parts of a rocket, engineers stack one rocket on top of another. Each rocket is called a stage.

In a multistage rocket, the first stage is the largest. It must lift itself, as well as all the stages above it, from Earth's surface. Once its fuel and oxidizer are used up, the first stage falls away and the next stage can start its engines. The second stage can be smaller than the first one because it only has to lift itself and the stages it carries. And as before, once its fuel and oxidizer are used up, it can be cast off. Each time an empty stage is dumped, the rocket becomes lighter and can go higher and faster. Stages can be stacked one atop the other, as in the Saturn V, or they can be mounted side by side, as on the space shuttle.

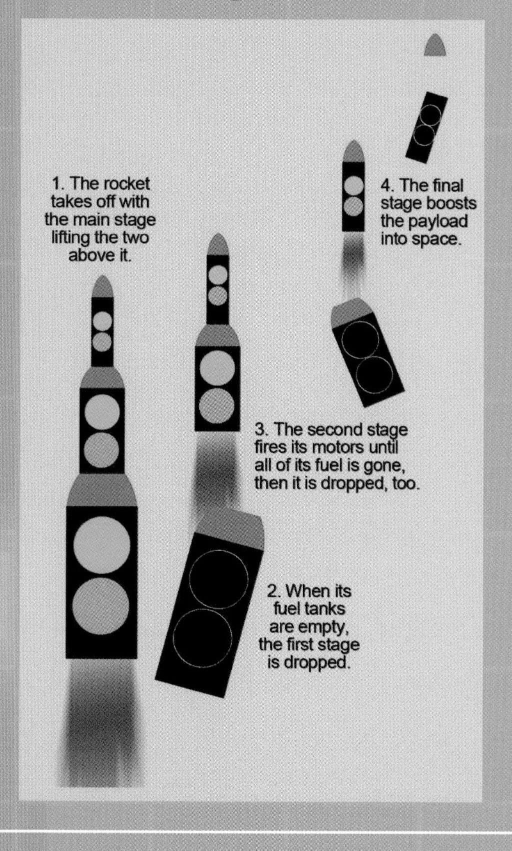


By discarding empty fuel tanks as it goes, the staged rocket is able to travel much farther and faster than a single-stage rocket of the same size.

Professor S. Fred Singer was the designer of MOUSE in the early 1950s. Although it was never launched into space, it paved the way for many of the techniques and instruments that were used in the first successful Earth satellites.

MOUSE turned out to be similar in shape, size, and function to many of the first successfully launched satellites.

Project Orbiter was one of the most interesting early proposals. Begun in 1954, it was a collaborative project involving the U.S. Navy, U.S. Army, and private industry. At that time, the various branches of the military had several high-altitude research programs. But there was no serious satellite program. When Wernher von Braun, who was in charge of the project, was asked if it would take as long as three years to get a satellite into orbit, he replied that he could do it sooner than that.

Von Braun planned to use an existing Juno 1 rocket. This was a modified version of the army's Redstone, which had in turn been developed by von Braun from the V-2. The Juno 1 would be the first stage of a multistage launch vehicle. The satellite it launched would be modest in size. It would weigh between 5 pounds (2.3 kg) and 15 pounds (6.8 kg), depending on how powerful the upper stages of the rocket would be. It was thought that if the project were given the go-ahead, a satellite could be sent into orbit by 1956.

Project Orbiter never made it off the ground. This was due in large part to rivalries within the navy itself. The Naval Research Laboratory had independently developed its own plan for a satellite, which it called Project Vanguard. Vanguard was a product of a scientific event called the International Geophysical Year (IGY). The IGY actually lasted for eighteen months—beginning on July 1, 1957—and involved the cooperation of fifty-four countries. The purpose of IGY was to explore planet Earth in detail. Earth satellites were required for this exploration.

Although IGY officially began in 1957, planning for it started many years in advance. When Project Orbiter was considered for its potential role in IGY, experts feared that its satellite would be too small to carry the necessary scientific instruments. A larger, heavier rocket would be needed. This new rocket would be the Vanguard.

An artist's depiction shows the *Vanguard 1* satellite in orbit. Although it carried batteries, the small, boxlike attachments are solar cells, which provided additional electrical power.

The announcement of the Vanguard satellite project was made two years before IGY began. The rocket would be developed largely from existing hardware. The first stage would be brand new, but the second stage would be a modified Aerobee-Hi sounding rocket (a rocket used to explore the upper atmosphere). The final stage would be a solid-fuel rocket developed from scratch especially for the project. The resulting slender, 70-foot (21 m) rocket would be superior to anything else that existed. Or so the designers hoped.

The satellites themselves would be gold-plated spheres weighing between 21 pounds (9.7 kg) and 99 pounds (45 kg). They would range in size from 6.4 inches (16 centimeters) to 20 inches (50 cm) in diameter. They would contain instruments for studying temperature, X-rays, Earth's magnetic field, and other subjects. While smaller and lighter than Singer's MOUSE, the Vanguard satellites clearly followed his pattern.

All of this looked good on the drawing board. Vanguard enjoyed nationwide publicity. Warnings from engineers and other experts that every Vanguard launch might not be successful—it was, after all, a totally untested new rocket—went unheeded. The navy was ready to give the project a green light when something unexpected happened.

## Red Star in Space

On October 4, 1957, the United States and the rest of the world were shocked to learn that the Soviet Union had launched the first artificial satellite. It was named *Sputnik 1* (*sputnik* is the Russian word for "companion" or "satellite"). It was an aluminum sphere 22 inches (56 cm) in diameter, weighing 184 pounds (83 kg). Although it contained scientific instruments, it is most famous for its radio signal. Its persistent *beep beep beep* was a constant reminder to its U.S. rivals that the Soviet Union had beaten them into space.

The United States immediately went into action. Project Orbiter was resurrected. Von Braun promised that, given the go-ahead, he could put a satellite into orbit in ninety days. Meanwhile, the U.S. Navy was no less anxious to get its Vanguard satellite into space. But before anyone could make a decision about which plan to go with, the Soviets

## Anatomy of the First Satellite

*Sputnik 1* was an example of just how simple a satellite could be. It contained few items: a battery, a thermometer, and a radio transmitter that changed the tone of its beeps to match changes in temperature. The interior of the satellite was pressurized with nitrogen gas to protect the contents. On the outside were four slender antennae that transmitted radio signals on shortwave frequencies above and below what is today's citizens band. After ninety-two days in orbit, *Sputnik 1* reentered Earth's atmosphere and burned up.

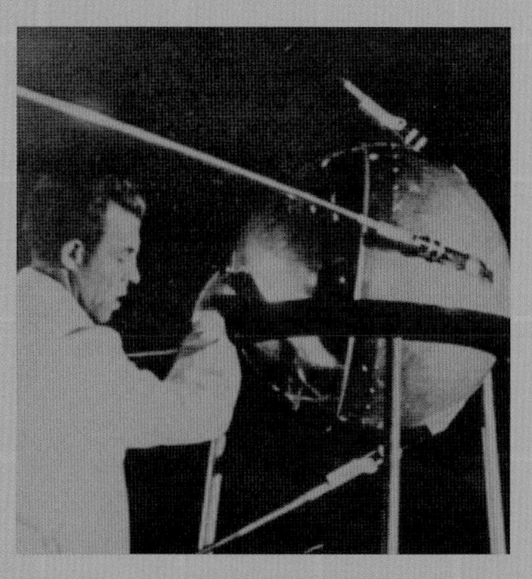

The Soviets' *Sputnik 1* satellite is being prepared for launch by a technician in 1957.

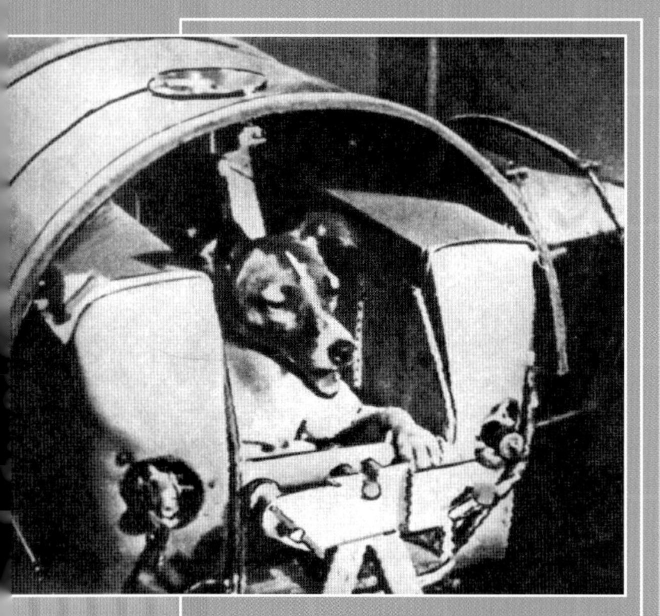

Laika, a Samoyed-terrier mix, was the first living creature to fly in space. Here she is in her capsule just before launch in 1957.

launched yet another satellite, *Sputnik 2*. This time the satellite was huge. It weighed more than 1,000 pounds (455 kg). And it carried a passenger: a dog named Laika (meaning "Barker").

In a panic, the navy rushed to launch a Vanguard satellite. The rocket had performed perfectly during two earlier suborbital tests. However, when the satellite launch was attempted, the rocket blew up spectacularly on the launchpad. The silvery satellite spilled from the wrecked rocket and rolled across the ground with its transmitter cheerfully beeping away. It was a national embarrassment. One newspaper headline announced, "What A Flopnik!"

Less than a week later, von Braun got the government approval he had been waiting for. And von Braun was better than his word.

The first attempt to launch a Vanguard rocket, on December 6, 1957, resulted in an explosion. Televised live across the world, this failure was an embarrassment to the United States.

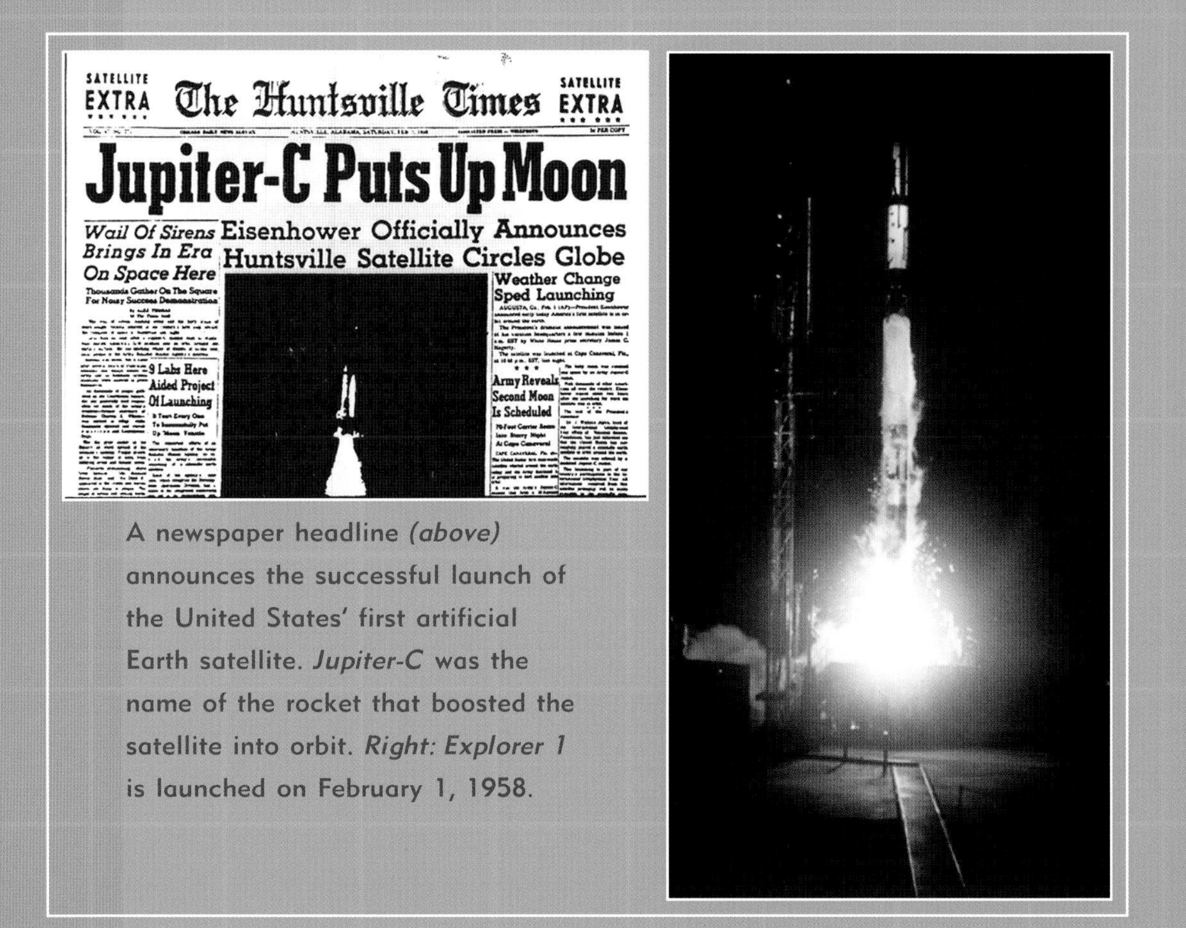

SATELLITE EXTRA

The Huntsville Times

SATELLITE EXTRA

# Jupiter-C Puts Up Moon

## Eisenhower Officially Announces Huntsville Satellite Circles Globe

### Wail Of Sirens Brings In Era On Space Here

Thousands Gather On The Square For Noisy Success Demonstration

### 9 Labs Here Aided Project Of Launching

### Weather Change Sped Launching

### Army Reveals Second Moon Is Scheduled

A newspaper headline *(above)* announces the successful launch of the United States' first artificial Earth satellite. *Jupiter-C* was the name of the rocket that boosted the satellite into orbit. *Right: Explorer 1* is launched on February 1, 1958.

Eighty-five days later, he placed *Explorer 1*, the United States' first artificial satellite, into orbit.

It wasn't much of a satellite compared to the monsters the Soviet Union had in space. *Explorer 1* was a cylinder less than 3 feet (1 m) long and 6 inches (15 cm) in diameter. But it was a huge step toward restoring American pride. And it was superior in only one way to the Soviet satellites. Although it was much smaller than the Sputniks, *Explorer 1* carried more scientific instruments. U.S. advances in miniaturization allowed powerful instruments to be made small and light. Eventually, this proved to be extraordinarily important.

The U.S. Navy, stung by the triumph of the army rocket, tried again to launch the Vanguard. Again, it failed spectacularly. The Vanguard rocket was just too new. Although it was based on the

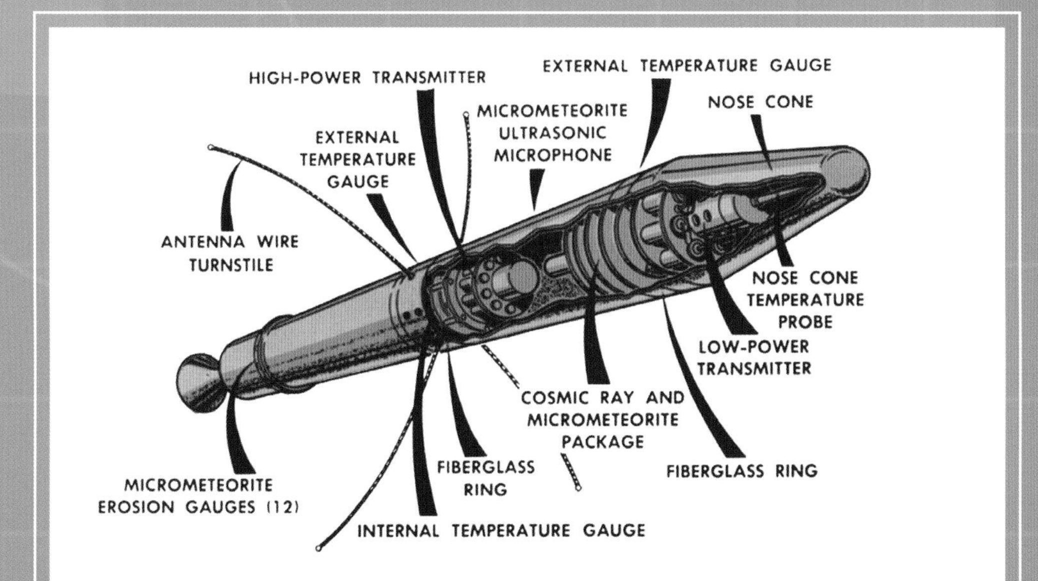


This cutaway view of *Explorer 1* shows all its instruments, which were designed and built by Dr. James Van Allen of the University of Iowa. The spacecraft itself was designed and built by the Jet Propulsion Laboratory of the California Institute of Technology.

successful navy Viking rocket, it was essentially a brand new design from nose to tail. And like any new design, it invariably did not work on its first try. Every stage of the army rocket, on the other hand, was built from proven components.

In eleven attempts to get its satellite into orbit, the navy succeeded only three times. The failures were enormously embarrassing—people throughout the world witnessed them on live television. However, the three successful launches proved to have great scientific value. Important discoveries were made about Earth and the conditions in space. Technical innovations developed, as well. For example, solar cells were used for generating electrical power in the satellite. The Sputniks and Explorer satellites all ran on batteries. The first successful Vanguard satellite, *Vanguard 1*, which was launched in 1958, is still in orbit in the 2000s, though it has long since lost power.

## The Space Race

The launch of the first Earth satellites marked the beginning of the space age—the age of space exploration. The greatest race in the history of humankind had begun. The race between two superpowers to outdo each other in the conquest of space ensued. It was to be known as the space race.

Between 1958 and 1961, four more Explorer satellites were launched. With the development of larger and more powerful launch vehicles, satellites weighing tons instead of pounds could be put into orbit. Satellites intended to perform specific roles could be launched, as well. For instance, *Telstar 1* was the first communications satellite and the satellites called TIROS (Television and Infrared Observation Satellite) were weather satellites.

Meanwhile, the Soviet Union was launching even more satellites into orbit. Most of these were involved in pure scientific research, but the Soviets launched communications satellites, as well. The Soviets were able to launch satellites that were much larger and heavier than those of the Americans because their launch vehicles were developed from military rockets. At that time, the Soviets' rockets were larger and more powerful than those of the West (the non-Communist countries of Europe and North America).

But Western engineers did not know at the time that the Soviets' main rocket was actually a cluster of engines. The rocket was complicated, heavy, and inefficient compared to the sleeker U.S. rockets, but it worked. The United States soon caught up, however, with its lighter-weight, more conventional, and more efficient launch vehicles. Some of them had single, double, or triple engines in their first stage.

# Getting into Space

So far, there has been only one way to get a satellite into orbit: launch it into space on the nose of a rocket. A rocket used for this purpose is called a launch vehicle, or booster. Since the mid-twentieth century, many rockets have been used as launch vehicles. Some of these rockets have been remarkable in their reliability, longevity, and numbers of satellites launched. A launch vehicle is different from other rockets because it can be used to launch many different types of payloads.

One of the earliest rockets for launching satellites, the Soyuz *(above)*, has been used in Russia since the early 1960s. Variations of it are still in use. It has been the backbone of Russia's boosters.

The U.S. Delta rocket series was created in the 1960s. It has proved to be one of the most successful and reliable launch vehicles in the world. Delta rockets *(below)* have launched hundreds of satellites, including TIROS, Nimbus, LANDSAT, and more than thirty scientific Explorer satellites. Deltas also placed the Global Positioning System satellites into orbit.

Like the Delta, the Atlas series of boosters originated from a rocket designed for the U.S. military in the 1960s. This powerful rocket could place a satellite weighing as much as 13,000 pounds (5,897 kg) into orbit. An Atlas booster placed U.S. astronaut John Glenn into

orbit in 1961. Atlas boosters also launched the Orbiting Astronomical Observatories (OAO), many communications satellites, and the Mars Mariner orbiters. Atlas boosters even launched the Mariner spacecraft that made flybys of Venus and Mercury, the Pioneers that made flybys of Jupiter and Saturn, and the Pioneers that orbited Venus. An Atlas *(above)* was used to send the *New Horizons* probe to Pluto in 2006. It boosted the spacecraft to a speed faster than any other object ever launched from Earth.

The United States has used the space shuttle to place numerous large satellites into orbit, including the Hubble Space Telescope *(below)*. Instead of being carried in a nose cone, satellites launched by the space shuttle are carried in the shuttle's cargo bay, which is large enough to carry a satellite as big as a school bus.

The French Ariane rocket family has proved to be one of the most successful commercial launch vehicles in the world. First launched in 1973, it can put a satellite as heavy as 9.5 tons (9.7 metric tons) into orbit. In 1985 an Ariane 1 sent the *Giotto* probe to rendezvous with Halley's comet. The most recent model, Ariane 4, accomplished more than one hundred flights with a success rate of more than 97 percent. The final launch was in February 2003, when it placed the communications satellite *Intelsat 907* into orbit. Ariane 4 was replaced by Ariane 5, which can carry heavier payloads.

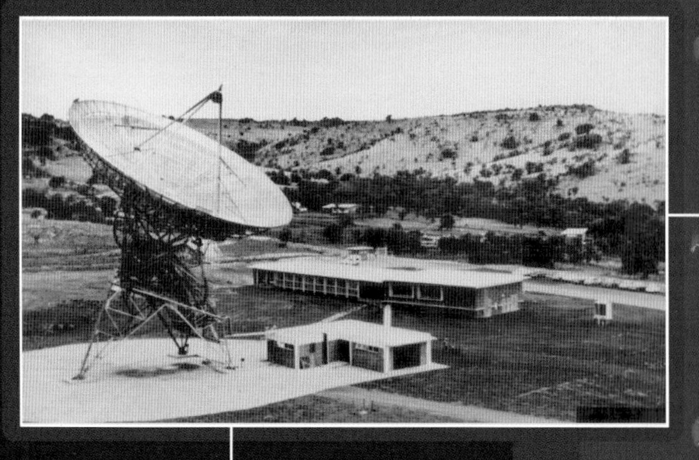

Satellites are nearly perfect instruments for observing the universe. They orbit far above the disruptive effects of Earth's atmosphere. They provide steady observations, far from such disturbances as earthquakes, traffic, and even the vibrations from human footsteps. Many satellites are studying the environment in which our planet exists. The first scientific satellites were meant to discover exactly what lies beyond Earth's atmosphere.

## The First Three Satellites

Of the first three Earth satellites launched—*Sputnik 1*, *Sputnik 2*, and *Explorer 1*—only the last two carried scientific instruments into space. Except for a Geiger counter that measured the levels of radiation in space, *Sputnik 2*'s instruments were devoted to measuring the reactions of the dog on board.

*Top:* A typical satellite tracking station receives signals broadcast from satellites in orbit. *Middle:* The Hubble Space Telescope was photographed from the space shuttle, with Earth in the background. *Bottom:* The Hubble Space Telescope took this photo of the center of the Orion Nebula, a glowing cloud of cosmic dust and gas.

*Explorer 1* carried Geiger counters as well as instruments for measuring the impacts of tiny meteorites and space dust. These instruments also kept track of internal and external temperatures. *Explorer 1* even carried a tape recorder. The recorder saved information for later transmission when it was passing over a receiving station on the ground below. *Explorer 1* circled Earth in a different orbit than *Sputnik 2*. This led to the first major discovery about Earth's environment by an artificial satellite.

The Geiger counters on *Explorer 1* revealed that the planet is surrounded by a pair of radiation belts. The belts are large, doughnut-shaped areas of intense radiation. They were named the Van Allen Belts after U.S. space scientist James Van Allen. Van Allen designed the instruments that discovered the belts. He was also the first scientist to recognize what the data from the Geiger counters meant.

This photo of Earth was taken in 1954 by an Aerobee sounding rocket (a rocket that makes observations within Earth's atmosphere). Images like this were of great importance to scientists. The images proved the need for permanently orbiting satellites, which could take such pictures continuously.

## "Satellites" on a Budget

The days of high-altitude balloon exploration are not over. It costs tens to hundreds of millions of dollars to place a satellite into orbit. But instruments can be carried to an altitude of more than 21 miles (34 km) with a balloon for a total investment of one thousand dollars or less.

At this altitude, nearly 99 percent of Earth's atmosphere lies below the balloon. Scientists consider near space to begin between 60,000 to 75,000 feet (18,288 and 22,860 m). It continues to 62 miles (100 km), where outer space begins. This means that simple balloons can gather data from altitudes nearly as high as the lowest-orbiting satellites. Unlike sounding rockets, they can keep their instruments aloft for hours at a time.

The Van Allen Belts were a complete surprise to scientists. The belts greatly worried the Soviet Union and the United States, who were at that time planning the first human flights into space. Would orbiting astronauts become sick or even die from the result of exposure to this radiation? While the radiation in the belts is intense

Receiving stations similar to this one in the United States are scattered all over the globe. Scientists at the stations listen to the signals broadcast from satellites in orbit.

enough to be dangerous to humans, astronauts' spacecraft pass through the belts too quickly for the astronauts to be harmed.

## New Eyes on the Sky

When you go outside on a clear night, it is hard to believe that anything exists between you and the thousands of twinkling stars overhead. But there is a hundred miles or more of various gases. These gases act like filters. They prevent a great deal of the stars' radiation from reaching Earth's surface. In many ways, this is a good thing. Large amounts of this radiation is dangerous to our health. On the other hand, the filtering process prevented scientists from learning more about radiation and the stars it comes from.

The twinkling light from the stars is also a source of interference when trying to observe the universe from the ground. The atmosphere is always moving, like the ocean. This movement distorts the rays of starlight that pass through the atmosphere. The distortion causes stars to appear to be twinkling. When magnified in a telescope, a star that should appear as a sharp point of light looks like a wiggling blob of colors.

Telescopic photographs of the planets are not much clearer than those of stars. The images astronomers try to capture are always moving because of the moving atmosphere, so photos always come out slightly blurred. This is the same thing that can happen in a photo of someone who is running.

For centuries this effect frustrated many astronomers. They could see fine, sharp details through their telescopes' eyepieces. This is because the human eye can record images lasting only a fraction of a second. So during those brief moments when the atmosphere is still, the eye can see sharp details. But those details disappeared in photos, which had to be taken with exposures lasting several seconds.

With the invention of satellites, the science of astronomy made great advances. Orbiting observatories allow astronomers to observe the universe from above the interference of Earth's atmosphere. This gave scientists a clarity that had never been seen in the past.

The National Aeronautics and Space Administration's (NASA) Orbiting Astronomical Observatories (OAO) were a series of four satellites launched between 1966 and 1972. They studied the ultraviolet and X-ray emissions of stars, the hydrogen halos around comets, and other things virtually impossible to observe from Earth's surface. For instance, OAO 3 (called *Copernicus*) discovered the first known black hole, Cygnus X-1, while measuring the black hole's X-ray radiation.

The Orbiting Astronomical Observatory was one of a series of four space observatories launched by NASA between 1966 and 1972. They provided the first high-quality observations of many objects in ultraviolet light.

# Orbits

Satellites do not typically orbit in neat circles above Earth's equator. In fact, an equatorial orbit is considered the least useful orbit of all. If a satellite is meant to observe as much of Earth as possible, a polar orbit is ideal. The satellite orbits over the North and South poles. As it orbits, Earth slowly rotates beneath it. The satellite passes over a different region of the planet every time it orbits. It eventually passes over every spot on the globe.

It is possible to arrange the timing of a polar orbit so that the satellite will pass over the same spot at the same time of day each month. This allows scientists to accurately chart changes in specific areas on Earth's surface. Satellites can also be placed into orbits that lie at any angle between 0 degrees, an equatorial orbit, and 90 degrees, a polar orbit.

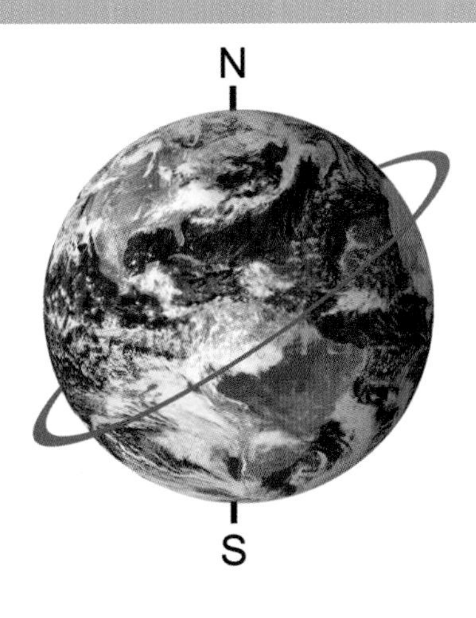


In an equatorial orbit *(top)*, the satellite circles Earth directly above the equator. In a polar orbit *(middle)*, the satellite circles the planet from pole to pole. A satellite in an inclined orbit *(bottom)* passes over more of Earth's surface than a satellite in an equatorial orbit but less than one in a polar orbit. Satellites in inclined orbits cannot see regions close to the poles.

## Satellites and the Sun

The Sun became a major subject of study by Earth satellites. Early satellites discovered solar wind. Solar wind consists of atomic particles—parts of atoms called electrons and protons—that are thrown away from the Sun at enormous speeds: between 200 and 350 miles per second (322 to 563 km/sec). This "wind" blows Earth's magnetic field into a teardrop shape. Solar wind also blows the tails of comets into long plumes.

Solar wind is the cause of the beautiful auroras that shimmer above the North and South poles. Like iron filings attracted to a magnet, solar particles spiral into the magnetic poles. There they slam into high-altitude molecules of Earth's atmosphere. This releases energy that we see in the form of shifting bands of light called auroras.

Satellites also studied the Sun's magnetic field and monitored solar storms and flares. Solar storms and flares cause huge bursts of

Atomic particles racing away from the Sun collide with Earth's magnetic field (purple and blue lines), distorting it like the tail of a comet. Earth's magnetic field acts as a kind of shield, protecting life on the planet from this radiation, which would be very dangerous if it reached the ground.

radiation to propel into space. This radiation can disrupt radio and television broadcasts on Earth.

The Sun is monitored constantly by satellites because it is our only opportunity to study a star up close. Other than the Sun, the nearest star—Alpha Centauri—is more than four light-years away. (A light-year is the distance light travels in one year. Light travels at a speed of 186,000 miles a second [300,000 km/s]. At four light-years away, this equals about 6 trillion miles [9.5 trillion km]. That makes Alpha Centauri about 27 trillion miles [43 trillion km] from the Sun). Even viewed through the largest telescopes, Alpha Centauri appears as only a tiny pinpoint of light. What scientists learn about the Sun helps them understand how other stars work. This leads to a better understanding of our galaxy and the universe in which it exists.

## Into the Universe

Since the 1990s, some of the most exciting and extraordinary astronomical discoveries have been made by the Hubble Space Telescope. The Hubble, named after U.S. astronomer Edwin Hubble (1889–1953), is really a kind of supersatellite.

The concept for an orbiting telescope goes back to 1946, more than ten years before the launch of the first artificial satellite. Although a space telescope was on the drawing boards from the beginning of the space age, technical, political, and budget problems delayed its launch for decades. The Hubble Space Telescope was finally launched from the space shuttle *Discovery* on April 25, 1990.

It was not clear when it was launched that the telescope was going to be as successful as it became. The first pictures that Hubble sent back were badly out of focus. It turned out that there was a major flaw in the giant 7.9-foot (2.4 m) primary mirror. The flaw had somehow slipped past every test conducted by NASA and the mirror's manufacturer. The mirror was too flat on one edge by one-fiftieth of the width of a single human hair. This sounds like practically nothing, but it was enough to ruin the photographs.

Three years after Hubble was launched, astronauts from the space shuttle *Endeavor* captured and modified the space telescope. They added a lens to correct the problems with the telescope's primary mirror. Each day Hubble has been in operation since then, the huge orbiting observatory generates 500 gigabytes of data. This is enough data to fill 106 DVDs. It is also enough information to fill every book in the Library of Congress. The Hubble Space Telescope has changed the course of astronomy.

Hardly a month has gone by since its launch without some fabulous photograph from Hubble appearing in the news. In June 1994, Hubble images of the Orion Nebula confirmed the births of planets around newborn stars. In January 1996, Hubble images allowed astronomers to peer back in time more than 10 billion years. The images revealed at least 1,500 galaxies at various stages in their development.

The telescope has allowed astronomers to fine-tune their estimates of the age of our universe. It had once been estimated to be

This Hubble Space Telescope image shows the center of the Orion Nebula. Located 1,500 light-years away from Earth, the Orion Nebula is the brightest spot in the sword of the Orion constellation. This glowing cloud of cosmic dust and gas is a nursery of newborn stars. Astronomers believe it contains more than one thousand young stars.

## The Hubble Time Machine

Light travels at the tremendous speed of 186,000 miles a second (300,000 km/s). At this speed, a beam of light can cross the United States in less than two-hundredths of a second. It would take the same beam a little more than one second to reach the Moon. Meanwhile, sunlight takes about eight minutes to travel from the Sun to Earth. This means that you are seeing the sunlight not as it is right now, but as it was eight minutes ago. Light from the nearest star, Alpha Centauri, takes a little more than four years to reach Earth. So if Alpha Centauri were to suddenly disappear, you wouldn't know it for another four years.

As astronomers look deeper and deeper into the universe—at objects farther and farther away—they are looking into the universe's past. When they observe a galaxy billions of light-years away, they are seeing that galaxy as it looked billions of years ago. If an object is distant enough, astronomers may be seeing what the universe looked like shortly after its creation. So a telescope like the Hubble is in a very real sense a time machine.

about 4 billion years old. New estimates say the universe formed nearly 14 billion years ago.

Hubble has also helped discover new solar systems beyond our own. Discovering planets around other stars has given scientists clues to how our solar system and our own planet formed. The Hubble even took close-up photos in 1994 when a comet slammed into Jupiter. Seeing the impact of a comet on another planet has given us graphic warning of one of the potential dangers facing Earth.

The Hubble Space Telescope has kept nearly six thousand astronomers from throughout the world busy with all of the amazing discoveries its photographs have made possible. Hubble has transformed our understanding of the universe more than any other scientific instrument ever created.

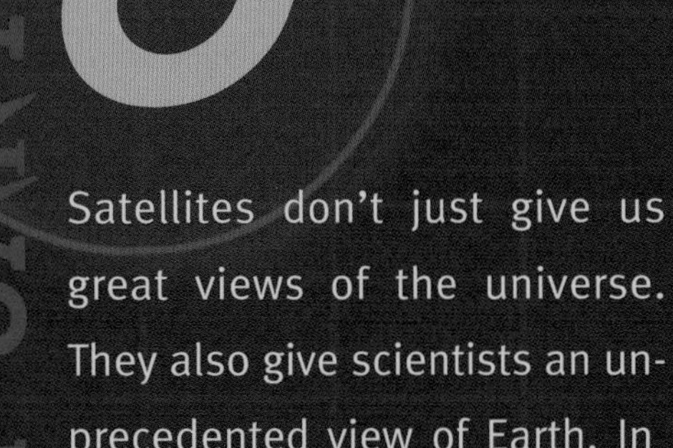

# 6 EYES ON EARTH

Satellites don't just give us great views of the universe. They also give scientists an unprecedented view of Earth. In the past, scientists were limited to what they could see from the ground or what could be photographed from high-flying aircraft. With satellites, scientists can monitor Earth's atmosphere, as well as entire countries, continents, and oceans at a single glance. With such a broad view, they are much better able to understand how Earth works.

## An Eye on the Weather

Before satellites were used to observe weather, meteorologists were limited to reports from manned and automatic stations scattered around the globe. Many of these stations were

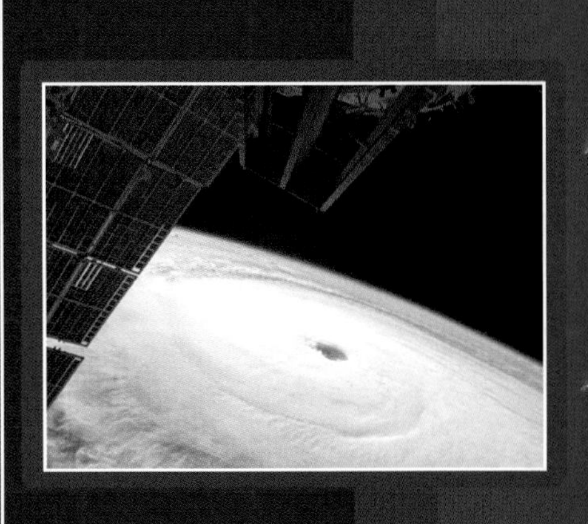

*Above*: Technicians prepare a TIROS weather satellite for launch. *Middle:* An artist's depiction shows a TIROS satellite as it would appear in orbit. *Bottom:* A hurricane with its eye was photographed by the crew of the International Space Station in 2004.

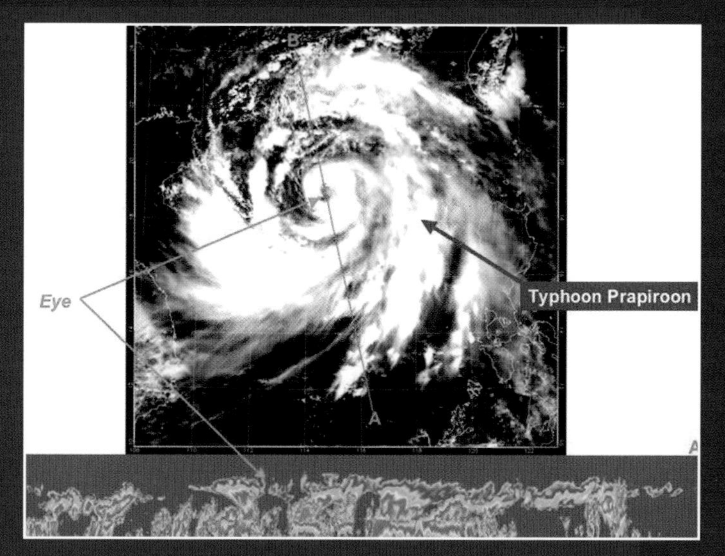


Photos from two different weather satellites were combined to create this image of Typhoon Prapiroon that hit China in 2006. The upper part of the photo came from NASA's *Aqua* satellite, while the lower part is from NASA's *CloudSat* satellite. The *CloudSat* flies behind the *Aqua* satellite, as part of a large group of satellites. In the image, the red and purple areas indicate large amounts of cloud water. The blue areas along the top of the clouds indicate cloud ice, while the wavy blue lines on the bottom indicate intense rainfall. The solid line along the bottom, which is the ground or ocean surface, disappears in many of these areas of intense precipitation. The *CloudSat* radar data can be processed to estimate the total amount of water and ice contained in this typhoon.

operated by amateurs who had their own weather-recording instruments. These amateurs regularly reported their findings to their government weather bureaus.

Although thousands of such stations are in place, remote areas of the planet still had no weather information available on a regular basis. Yet the remote areas were among the most important locations. These areas included the deserts, the poles, and the broad open regions of the oceans. It is the latter, for instance, where hurricanes and typhoons form that can cost hundreds of lives and billions of dollars in damage. But information about weather systems over the oceans was sparse or nonexistent. Meteorologists on land didn't know that a hurricane was brewing until it was nearly fully formed.

This problem was compounded by a lack of rapid communication. By the time weather data was received, processed, and distributed, people in the areas that would be affected had only a few hours' warning to prepare. A way to obtain better, more detailed weather data was needed. Meteorologists also needed a way to gather and distribute information quickly and efficiently, especially in time of emergency.

Satellites solved all of these problems. The first satellites used for monitoring weather conditions were a series launched by the United States called TIROS. The first TIROS was sent into orbit in 1960. Nine more were sent during the following five years. Each satellite carried a small television camera that beamed images of cloud patterns back to Earth. They also carried instruments for measuring the amount of solar radiation absorbed and reemitted by the planet.

*Left:* Technicians test and prepare a TIROS weather satellite for launch. *Middle:* An artist's depiction shows a TIROS satellite as it would appear in orbit. Its main mission was to photograph Earth's weather systems from orbit. The first TIROS contained two television cameras and a tape recorder, which were used to store data until the satellite could pass over a ground receiving station. *Right:* This photo taken by TIROS in 1960 is one of the earliest weather satellite images of Earth. It appears crude compared to the high-resolution images available from modern weather satellites, but images such as this provided detailed information about the planet's weather systems that had never before been available.

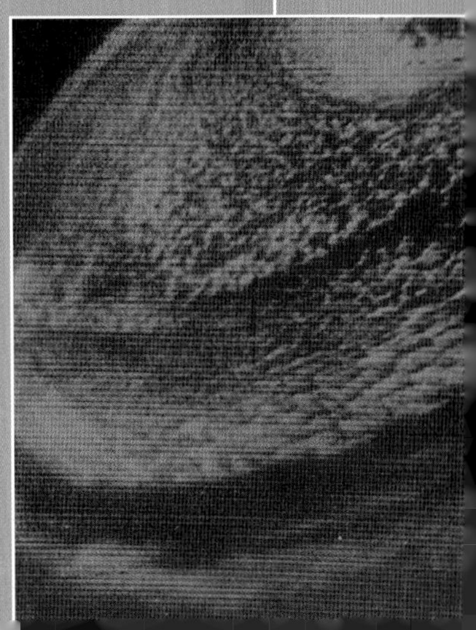

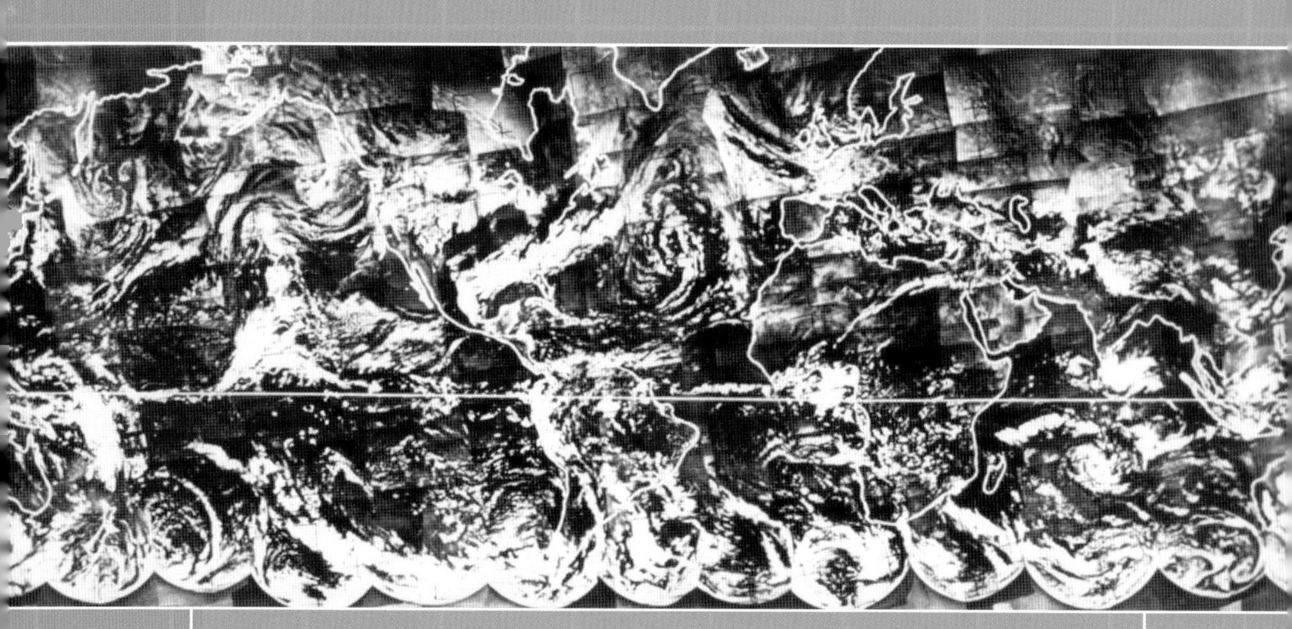

The weather system of the entire Earth was seen for the first time in this historic image that was created from a large number of separate TIROS images in 1965.

## Avoiding Disaster

Weather satellite coverage has grown dramatically. The entire planet is continually photographed at least once a day. Modern weather satellites return a vast amount of information to Earth. Meteorologists can study large-scale formations in the atmosphere. Visible-light images give scientists information about clouds, cloud systems such as fronts and tropical storms, snow, fires, and pollution such as smoke, smog, dust, and haze. Wind direction can be determined by cloud patterns and by comparing photos taken over periods of time. Even the amount of ice cover surrounding the polar regions can be monitored.

Weather satellites also carry instruments sensitive to wavelengths beyond human detection. Infrared detectors, for instance, can measure the temperatures of land and water. They can also be used to determine cloud heights and types or to detect swirling movements in the oceans called eddies and vortices. Infrared detectors map currents such as the Gulf Stream.

Once a storm, such as a hurricane, is discovered, the satellites can be used to track it. By knowing the past course of the storm, meteorologists can predict its future path. This gives people sufficient warning to save lives and property.

Hurricane Katrina in 2005, for example, was first discovered by satellites when the storm was still far out to sea. Satellites operated by the National Oceanographic and Atmospheric Administration (NOAA) tracked Katrina from beginning to end. The NOAA gave advance warning about the development, approach, and strength of the hurricane. This contributed significantly to the near 80 percent evacuation rate of New Orleans, Louisiana.

Hurricane watches and warnings for Louisiana, Mississippi, Alabama, and the Florida Panhandle gave citizens anywhere from eight

Hurricane Ivan was photographed by the crew of the International Space Station in 2004.

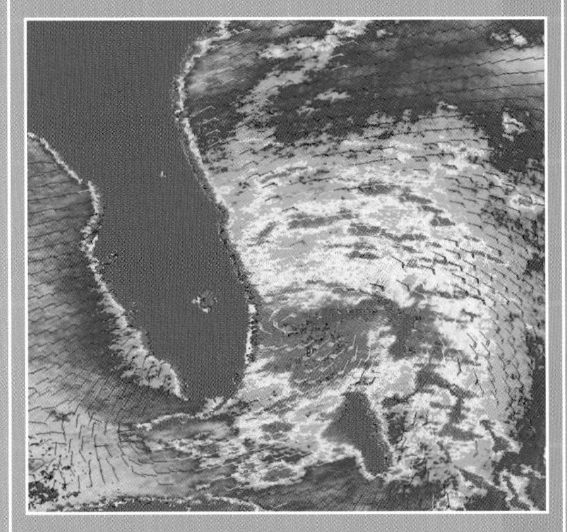

Tropical Storm Katrina is shown here as observed by NASA's *QuikSCAT* satellite on August 25, 2005, as it reached the coast of Florida. At this time, the storm had not yet achieved hurricane strength. The image shows wind speed in color and wind direction with small arrows.

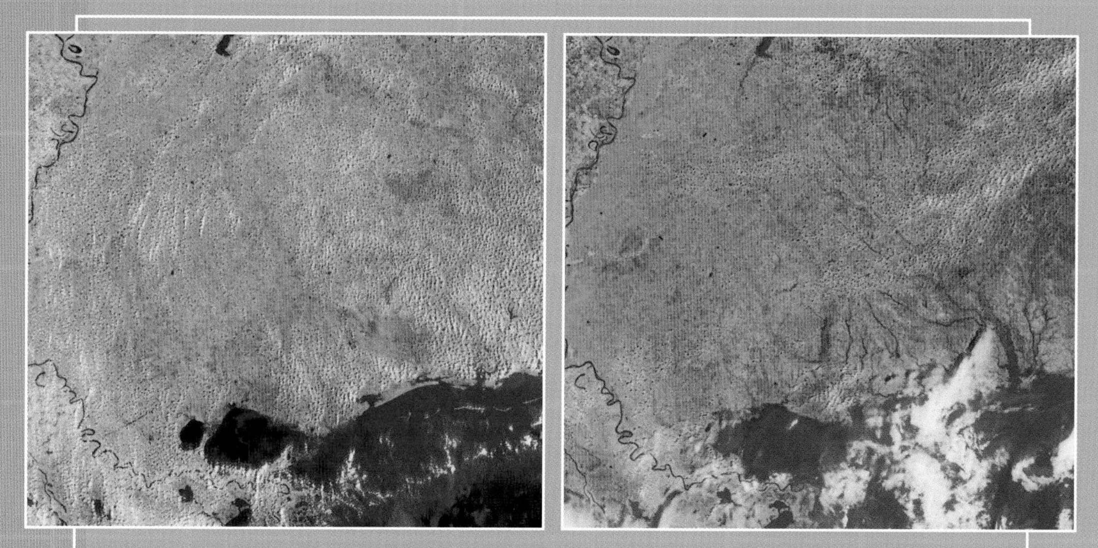

The extent of the flooding caused by Hurricane Katrina in 2005 is visible in these two satellite images, one taken before the storm and one immediately after. The purple areas show land covered by water.

hours to several days to prepare or evacuate. Thousands of lives were saved. After the storm, satellites enabled environmental scientists, rescue workers, and other officials to assess the extent of flooding and the damage it caused.

This type of information is also used by environmental scientists, who can measure and track water pollution. Satellites have proved invaluable in tracking oil spills in the oceans. The damage to animals and shorelines can be reduced, and spills are easier to clean up.

Satellites also monitor air pollution. Instruments can measure the amount of carbon dioxide, carbon monoxide, and other greenhouse gases being emitted by cars, industry, and natural sources such as volcanoes.

## Farming from the Sky

Agriculture, too, derives practical benefits from satellites. Both farmers and fishers are interested in knowing land and water temperatures. This information helps farmers to protect their crops against

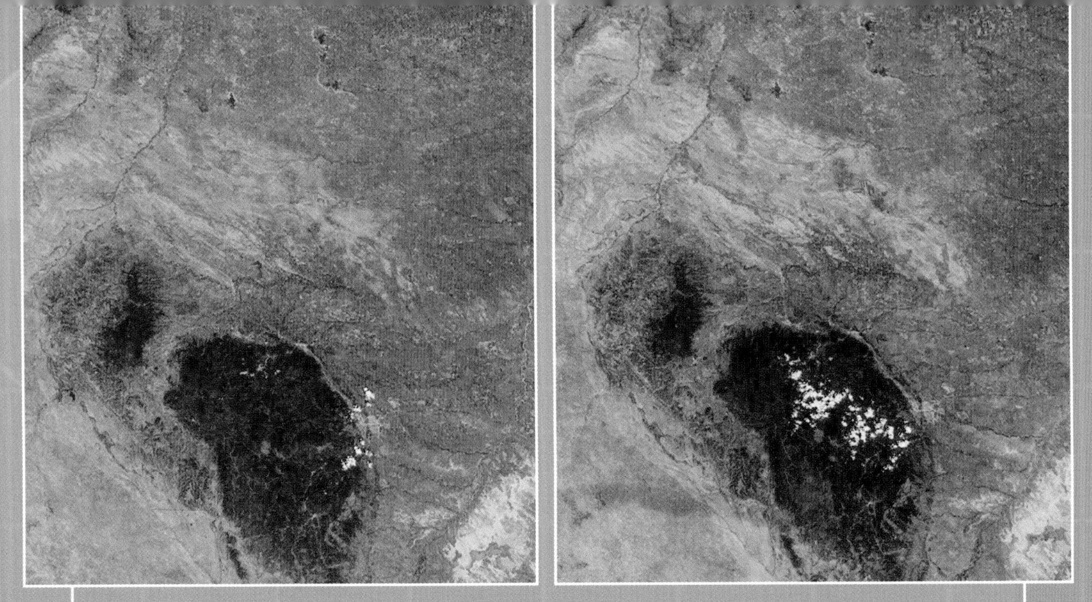

Despite good rainfall and record-setting snowstorms in spring 2005, most of northeastern Wyoming, the Black Hills of South Dakota, and western South Dakota remained in the middle of a severe drought. This set of images from a NASA Earth observation satellite contrasts the appearance of the Black Hills region of northwestern South Dakota on July 12, 2000 *(left)*, with views taken four years later *(right)*. The browning that appears in the 2004 photo shows that the amount of green vegetation had been significantly reduced.

frost and increases fishers' catches from the sea.

Satellite photos taken from space allow scientists to calculate the total acreage of various crops. By comparing this information with past measurements and combining it with meteorological records, accurate predictions of crop yields can be made.

Satellite images are even able to distinguish among different types of crops. Scientists can tell whether a field is planted with wheat, soy, corn, tomatoes, lettuce, or almost any other type of crop. Plots as small as 1 acre (0.4 hectare) can be distinguished. By being able to keep an accurate watch on crops, scientists can help prevent catastrophic food shortages and avoid overplanting one crop and underplanting another.

Satellites can also monitor the condition of the soil and its moisture content. Combined with information from meteorological satellites, scientists can warn farmers of impending drought conditions.

Satellites can keep an eye on snowmelt. This enables scientists to predict potential flood conditions. It also shows the amount of water available for crop irrigation and power generation. Similar measurements can track the progression of frost. This gives farmers advance warning of potential danger to their crops, which can result in saving millions of dollars in damaged fruits and vegetables.

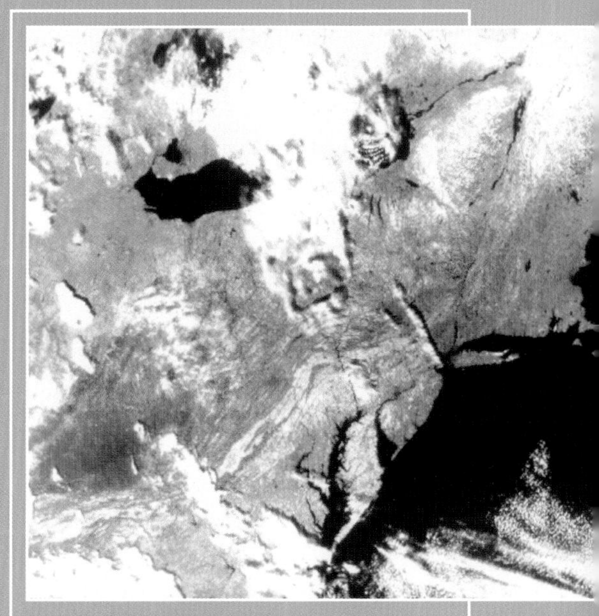

A NOAA satellite took this image of the northeastern United States in winter 1994. It not only reveals the extent of cloud cover but the amount of snow on the ground, as well. This is important in predicting how much snowmelt to expect in the spring, which in turn allows scientists to predict possible flooding.

## Natural Resources

Forests can be monitored from space just as farms can. Information gathered from satellites tells foresters the best time to plant new trees and harvest old ones. This helps them achieve the maximum yield.

The total amount of timber available on a tree farm can be accurately measured so that overcutting won't occur. Rangelands where cattle, sheep, and other animals are raised can be monitored to reduce damage to the land by overgrazing.

Satellite imagery can also be useful in the case of forest fires. Satellites can help firefighters monitoring wind conditions to predict the path a fire may take. It is also easy to determine the extent of damage to the land after the fire has been extinguished when the area is viewed from space.

These LANDSAT images taken in 2006 show an area in Southern California before *(left)* and after *(right)* damage caused by wildfires.

Satellite data has also proven to be invaluable in the discovery and development of mineral resources. By studying satellite imagery, geologists can decipher the surface signs of underground oil or natural gas. Minerals can be detected by the colors of the landscape and by characteristic geological formations. Searching for oil and minerals from space saves hundreds of hours of searching on foot or from the air. It has also enabled the oil and mining industries to discover billions of dollars' worth of new resources that may not have been found otherwise.

## Eyes on the Oceans

The oceans can also be observed in detail from space. Currents are traced, and water temperatures are monitored. Waves are photographed, ice fields are measured, icebergs are tracked, and coastlines are watched for erosion.

Global warming—which many scientists believe is caused by gases such as carbon dioxide trapping the Sun's heat—is causing glaciers to shrink, the polar ice caps to melt, and ocean levels to rise.

Keeping track of these changes is important. For instance, in early 2007, a huge 171-square-mile (443 sq. km) ice shelf broke away from the Arctic ice cap. Scientists were able to observe this event with satellite imagery. Huge free-floating ice islands such as this one could pose a danger to shipping and drilling platforms in the northern seas.

Since the polar ice is freshwater, its breaking up and melting changes the balance of salt water in the surrounding seas. This creates changes in the environment of the sea life. Many creatures are highly sensitive to changes in the salt content of seawater. Some of the organisms that may not survive these changes are the basic food source for thousands of other species.

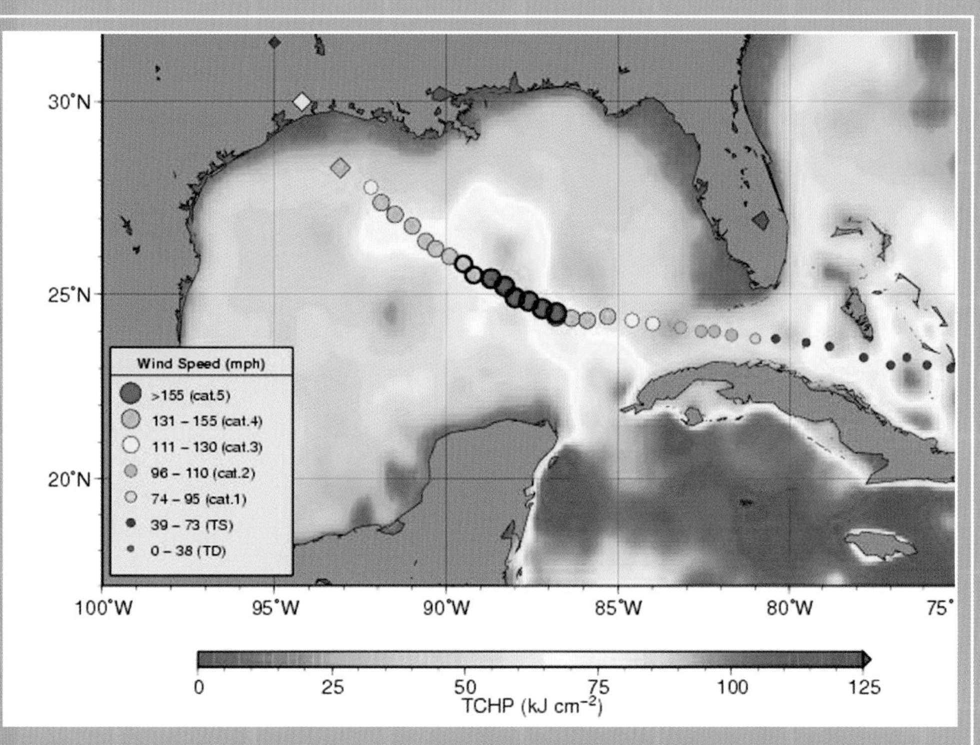


Data gathered from weather satellites allows scientists to monitor ocean water temperatures. This is important since warm waters provide the energy that powers storms, such as hurricanes. In this image, we see the ocean temperatures and wind speeds for Hurricane Rita in 2005. Notice that the highest wind speeds (red dots) occurred when the storm passed over warm waters (yellow and orange areas) in the Gulf of Mexico.

Information from oceanographic satellites is vital to the fishing industry. El Niño, for instance, is a current of warm water that flows south along the coast of Ecuador. It can, however, flow as far south as Peru. When this happens, the warm waters kill vast numbers of fish. This in turn severely hurts the local fishing industries. Satellite data can help predict shifts in the current and save the fishers billions of dollars.

Satellite data can also provide fishers information about where they would most likely be able to find certain types of fish—such as salmon or tuna. This increases their catches and profits.

Keeping track of currents can save the shipping industry many millions of dollars in other ways. By taking advantage of a current heading in the same direction as the ship—or avoiding one heading in the opposite direction—shipowners can save money because the ships require less fuel. This saves fuel itself and reduces the amount of pollution caused by burning it.

## A Star to Steer By

Until the middle of the twentieth century, ships at sea were steered by a navigator's sure knowledge of the position of the stars and constellations. In modern times, ships and aircraft are still guided by stars but stars of a very different kind. It is a new constellation composed of twenty-four artificial satellites. These satellites compose part of the Global Positioning System (GPS).

The idea for the GPS first came to light in the early 1950s. The U.S. Air Force asked Dr. Ivan Getting of the Raytheon Corporation if he could develop a guidance system that could be used together with a new ballistic missile. The air force planned to launch this missile from specially designed railroad cars, so the location of its launch site would constantly be changing. But if the exact location of the launch could not be determined ahead of time, it would be impossible to aim the rocket at its target. It would be like a blindfolded person trying to hit a target with an arrow that was shot from a moving car.

Getting's solution was to use a system of satellites. The idea was based on the Loran (Long-Range Navigation) system that had been developed during World War II. Loran allowed pilots to locate the position of their aircraft by measuring the difference in time it took to receive signals from different radio stations. Loran, however, could allow pilots to determine their position in only two dimensions: latitude and longitude.

With a satellite system, pilots could find their position in three dimensions: latitude, longitude, and altitude. The principle was the same as Loran. The difference in time it took for radio signals to be received from the different satellites allowed navigators to compute their precise location.

Beginning in the mid-1950s, the U.S. Navy experimented with this idea with its Transit system of satellites, developed for Polaris submarines. That system was composed of six satellites—the first of which was launched in 1959—circling Earth in polar orbits. By measuring the Doppler shift of radio signals from the satellites, submarine navigators could locate their position to within fifteen minutes of longitude and latitude.

The development of a new satellite system moved quickly after this. In the late 1960s, the air force backed the Aerospace Corporation's development of a satellite positioning system. Meanwhile, the navy worked on its own system, called Timation. The army worked on a system called SECOR. Eventually, in 1968 the U.S. Department of Defense established a committee to coordinate all the various satellite navigation systems into one standard system.

Experiments in which scientists used mock "satellites" were

## Doppler Effect

The Doppler effect was named for the scientist Christian Doppler (1803–1853), who was the first to describe it. The Doppler effect is observed whenever any source of waves—sound, light, or radio—is moving with respect to an observer. If the source is moving toward you, there is an apparent upward shift in frequency. If the source is moving away, there is an apparent downward shift in frequency. You have experienced a Doppler shift when a police car or emergency vehicle siren is traveling toward you. As the vehicle approaches, the pitch of the siren sound is high. As it passes, the pitch of the siren becomes low. The amount by which the frequency of a wave shifts depends on the speed of the object producing or reflecting the wave. Therefore, scientists can measure the speed of an object with great accuracy by determining the amount of Doppler shift.

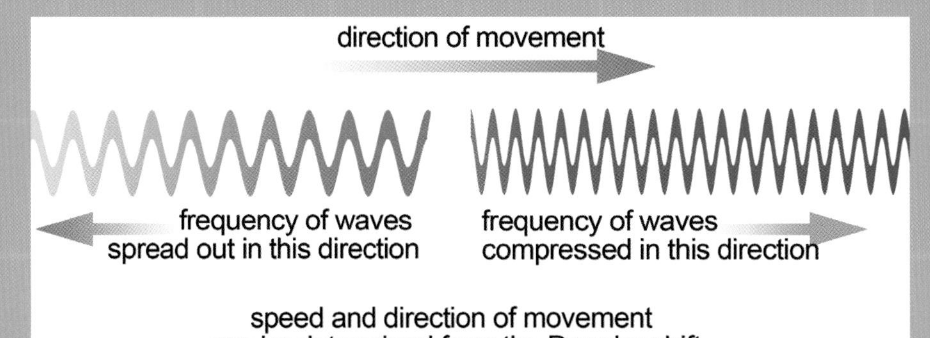


The wavelength of light emitted by a moving object is shifted. This effect is called the Doppler shift. If an object is coming toward you, the light coming from it is shifted toward shorter, bluer wavelengths. If the object is traveling away from you, the light coming from it is shifted toward longer, redder wavelengths.

performed in 1971 and 1972 in New Mexico. These were essentially little more than small radio transmitters carried by balloons. A receiver on the ground measured the distance to each balloon by timing how long it took its radio signal to arrive.

These tests showed that positions could be determined to within 0.01 mile (0.016 km). Satisfied with how things were going, the

Department of Defense proposed creating a single navigational system that could be used by all branches of the military. It was to be known as the Defense Navigational Satellite System (DNSS) and was to be overseen by the air force.

By 1973 the best of all the different systems had been combined into one system called NAVSTAR. NAVSTAR would consist of twenty-four satellites each orbiting Earth once every twelve hours. The first NAVSTAR satellite was launched on July 14, 1974. The complete system was in orbit and operating soon after.

NAVSTAR gave the U.S. military the ability to navigate with extreme precision. The military could also determine the location of a ship or aircraft to within a few yards. Of course, this was limited strictly to military use. Civilians could not take advantage of it. But in 1983, it became clear that a global positioning system might be of vital use to civilians.

In September of that year, a Korean airliner was shot down by the Soviets when it accidentally strayed into Soviet airspace. This incident prompted U.S. president Ronald Reagan to offer to make the military GPS available to civilian aircraft, free of charge. In 1991 the United States offered to make GPS

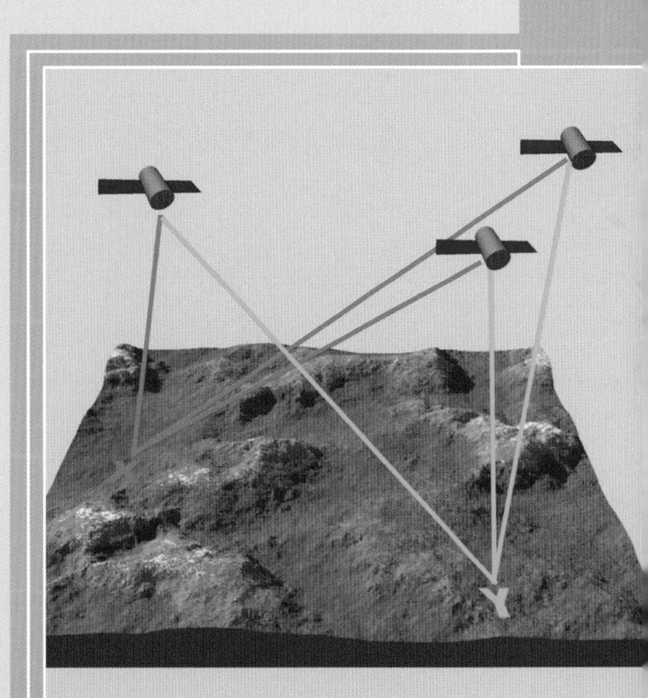


By measuring the distances to the known positions of at least three GPS satellites, a GPS receiver can calculate its location on the surface of Earth. The different distances of X and Y from the satellites means they are located at different places.

available to the entire world, beginning in 1993. GPS was offered at no charge for at least ten years. In 1992 the offer was extended indefinitely. This availability inspired all sorts of nonmilitary uses of the GPS. Surveyors were among the first to make use of the system, since an important part of their job is determining the precise location of points on Earth.

## The New Compass

GPS can be found everywhere. Able to pinpoint a location to within 6 feet (1.8 m), GPS receivers can be used to accurately track automobiles and other vehicles. If a vehicle's chassis number is part of the signal, then individual vehicles can be tracked. Police have found this technology invaluable in locating stolen cars.

Car manufacturers can use GPS to alert drivers when their cars are due for maintenance. The GPS relays information such as the status of the engine and the time since the last service. Then a computerized receiver decides what kind of alert to pass on to the driver. By knowing where an individual car is, the system can even inform the driver where the nearest service center is located.

GPS games have become very popular. In one game, called geocaching, players must locate a treasure hidden somewhere on the planet using their own handheld GPS devices.

Long-distance trucking companies use GPS to keep track of the locations of their vehicles. They can follow the routes of individual trucks to schedule pickups and deliveries. They can even tell where a driver stops and for how long. The systems also allow drivers to alert their headquarters in case of emergency.

GPS has enabled U.S. cities and counties to enhance their 911 emergency response systems. This allows first responders to accurately locate an injured person or other emergency. With GPS built into cell phones, people with cell phones can make emergency calls from almost anywhere.

Scientists have found many uses for GPS. For instance, if GPS devices are placed at certain locations, tiny changes in the movement of Earth's crust can be measured. These measurements enable researchers to better understand earthquakes and volcanoes. Even amateur astronomers are finding uses for GPS. Some new telescopes can find astronomers' exact location on Earth. These telescopes are powered by an onboard computer and motor drive. They can automatically locate certain stars and accurately track them through the sky.

Individuals are finding ever-increasing uses for GPS devices. Beyond the relatively small cost of the receiver itself, there are no subscription fees or setup charges. Hikers, fishers, and other outdoor enthusiasts use GPS because the devices are small, portable, and inexpensive. GPS devices can record the location of a favorite fishing spot or guide a hiker to her destination.

GPS devices can even track individual human beings. Miniature GPS units can be attached to children. Parents can find out where their children are at any time. Some units even sound an alert when the child crosses a predetermined boundary. In a similar way, GPS-equipped cell phones can be used to track their owners. The criminal justice system uses similar devices to keep track of convicted criminals whose sentences forbid them to wander past a certain distance from their homes.

# 7

# VOICES FROM THE SKY

GPS was not the only civilian application of satellites that had its origins in the military. The military has a great need for fast, long-range communications. This is especially true in an age when armies and navies might find themselves anywhere on the planet, thousands of miles away from their central commands.

Radio signals travel in straight lines. If a receiver is over the horizon, it cannot pick up a signal except under very special conditions. This is one of the reasons television and radio stations have such tall antennae. The higher the point being broadcast from, the farther the broadcast can be heard.

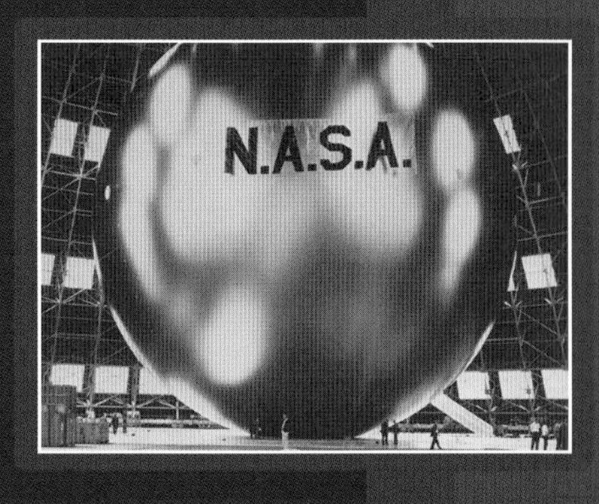


Another potential solution was to use relay stations that can pass signals from one station to another. But there are problems with relay stations. Dozens or even hundreds need to be built in order to cover a large area with radio signals. To get a signal across the world, stations would have to be built in many different countries. It is also difficult or impossible to establish permanent stations at sea. Communication directly between points thousands of miles apart seemed to be almost impossible.

*Above: Telstar 1* was the first communications satellite. *Middle:* The *Echo* satellite was really just a giant, 200-foot (61 m) balloon. *Bottom:* The Galactic Radiation and Background (GRAB) satellite was the first true "spy" satellite.

## Communicating with the World

British science-fiction writer Arthur C. Clarke had an influential idea in the mid-twentieth century. He knew that the larger a satellite's orbit, the slower it will travel. For example, a satellite traveling only 100 miles (161 km) or so above Earth's surface might circle the globe in only ninety minutes. The Moon, which is 234,000 miles (376,586 km) away, takes nearly a month to orbit once.

Clarke realized that if a satellite were to orbit just 22,300 miles (35,888 km) away, it would take exactly twenty-four hours to make one orbit. Since this is the same time it takes Earth to rotate once on its axis, the result would be amazing. The satellite would seem to hover motionless directly above one spot on the planet! A satellite that does this is said to be in a geosynchronous orbit (or geostationary orbit). This means that its orbit is synchronized with the rotation of Earth, so the position of the satellite remains fixed relative to one spot on the planet.

Clarke suggested placing three satellites into geosynchronous orbit. If the satellites orbited 120 degrees apart, radio signals from them would be able to reach every point on the globe. Therefore, a signal sent to one satellite from anywhere on the planet could be relayed to any other place almost instantly. Clarke's suggestion, however, was a little ahead of its time. In the 1950s, There was no way to get a satellite into orbit . . . yet.

## The Telstar Series

The U.S. military was the first to show interest in developing communications satellites. Military leaders realized very soon that in addition to observing, satellites could also be used for communications. Information can be quickly sent between almost any two places on Earth by bouncing the signals from satellites orbiting far overhead.

## Geosynchronous Orbits

Geosynchronous orbits are vital to communications satellites. A satellite in such an orbit will appear to "hover" above a point on Earth's surface. It is not easy to get a satellite into a geosynchronous orbit. It is also not easy to keep it there.

The satellite is usually launched by a rocket into a relatively low orbit around Earth. Once everything is in working order, the satellite is boosted by a smaller rocket into the much higher geosynchronous orbit. Satellites placed there, however, have a tendency to drift out of place. The effect of the Moon's gravity, for instance, is much greater on a satellite orbiting at such a great distance from Earth. A geosynchronous satellite must be given periodic nudges by small onboard rockets to keep it in place.

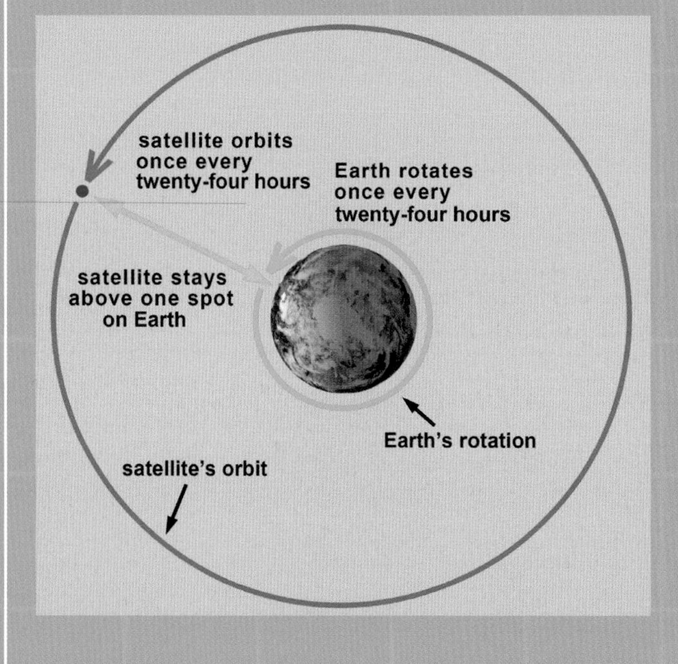


A satellite in geosynchronous orbit stays above one spot on Earth's surface. This is because the satellite takes just twenty-four hours to circle Earth. This is the same amount of time Earth takes to make one revolution on its axis.

If a satellite is not in a convenient location to bounce a signal directly back to a specific location on the ground, it can record the signal for transmission later. In fact, communications satellites were first developed by the military just as the GPS was.

In 1951 the U.S. Army bounced a radio signal off Earth's Moon. This was hardly a practical application of Clarke's idea. The army still needed a satellite in orbit, as well as electronics small enough and powerful enough to handle two-way communications. This dilemma was solved in 1962 with the launch of *Telstar 1*.

*Telstar 1* was placed in geosynchronous orbit with one of NASA's Delta launch vehicles. This satellite was the world's first communications satellite. And since it was paid for by the American Telephone & Telegraph Company (AT&T), it was the first commercial satellite, as well. A year later, *Telstar 2* was also placed in geosynchronous orbit. The first broadcast from space—seen by viewers in Great Britain, France, and the United States—featured a waving U.S. flag. This was soon followed by the first transatlantic telephone–television calls, in which specially equipped telephones allowed users to see the person they were talking to.

In 1962 *Telstar 1 (left)* became the first active communications satellite. The *Echo* satellite was passive, which means that signals only bounced off it. *Telstar 1*, on the other hand, processed the signals it received and retransmitted them. It was the first satellite designed to transmit telephone and high-speed data communications.

# The Echo Project

One of the first experiments using satellites in communications was launched into orbit on May 13, 1960. The *Echo* satellite bore a remarkable resemblance to Edward Everett Hale's fictional satellite, the Brick Moon. *Echo* was nothing more than a huge, silvery balloon. It was a perfect sphere 100 feet (30 m) in diameter, just half the size of the Brick Moon.

Unlike Hale's fictional satellite, Echo was made of extremely thin Mylar plastic. This allowed it to be folded up into a very small space when it was launched. Once in space, gas was used to inflate the satellite.

*Echo* contained no instruments. Its sole purpose was to act like a big mirror, reflecting radio, telephone, and television signals. The satellite was very large compared to its extremely light weight. Its light weight helped scientists calculate atmospheric density and solar pressure, since even the slightest resistance created enough pressure to affect the satellite's movement and position.

*Echo*'s shiny surface was also highly reflective. The satellite was visible to the unaided eye from all over Earth. It was brighter than most stars and probably seen by more people than any other manmade object in space. All one needed to know was where to look (most daily newspapers gave that information). *Echo* looked like a bright, slowly moving star. Since *Echo* was only a test project, it was allowed to reenter Earth's atmosphere, where it burned up on May 24, 1968.

The *Echo* satellite was really little more than a vast inflated sphere, like a beach ball or balloon. Its smooth, shiny aluminum-coated surface allowed radio waves to be reflected from it. *Echo* was so large and bright that it could easily be seen from the surface of Earth by the unaided eye.

The success of *Telstar 1* (which was really only a test of the basic concept) led to the launch of a full-scale communications satellite system. This system allowed television viewers in the United States to watch a live broadcast of the opening ceremony of the 1964 Summer Olympics in Tokyo, Japan. Following this event, the International Telecommunications Satellite Organization (Intelsat) was founded the same year. Its formation was inspired by the late president John F. Kennedy. Kennedy had said that all nations should "participate in a communications satellite system in the interest of world peace and closer brotherhood among people throughout the world."

Intelsat is owned and operated by its member nations. More than one hundred nations are involved, including many developing countries. The first satellite launched by the organization was *Intelsat 1*, which went into orbit in 1965.

## Connecting the World

The first domestic telecommunications satellites were created in the 1970s. Canada used a series of satellites called Anik (an Inuit word meaning "little brother") to link remote towns and villages. Indonesia and other nations soon followed suit. Before this, such communities had no way to communicate directly with one another or the outside world.

In the United States, the Western Union company began relaying television signals via its *Westar 1* satellite. By the late 1970s, cable television companies were using satellites to relay signals from city to city. Not long after this, receivers were made small enough to fit into the average backyard. Ordinary citizens gained the ability to pick up television signals directly from satellites.

The receivers were not cheap, however. Only relatively wealthy citizens could afford them. But by 1984, prices for home satellite receivers had dropped from more than ten thousand dollars to one thousand

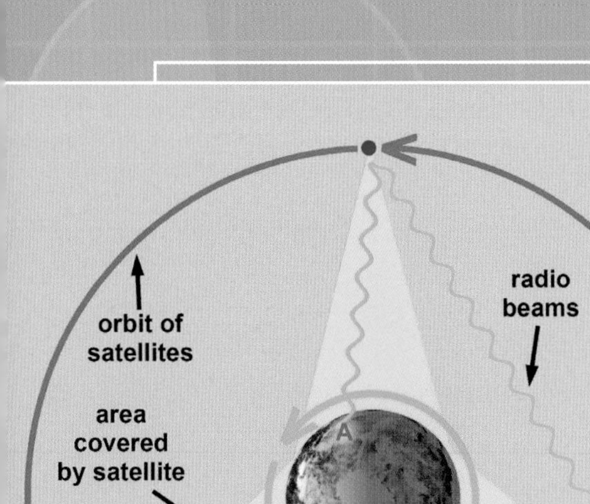


Telecommunications satellites take advantage of geosynchronous orbits to allow worldwide communications services, such as television, telephone, and the Internet. A person at A can talk to a person at B by transfering their call from one satellite to another.

dollars or less. Soon dish-shaped antennae started springing up everywhere. Providing homes and businesses with satellite television has become a multi-billion-dollar-a-year business.

Satellites have done more than make international communications or satellite television possible. Specialized satellite systems have brought educational programs to third world countries. Antennae can be cheaply and easily constructed from available materials such as wood and chicken wire. Inexpensive receivers are used. Information about health, farming, and other subjects is provided to people who may not have any other source of education. Such systems have been extremely valuable in India and many African countries.

Similar systems have allowed doctors to diagnose diseases and injuries in patients hundreds or even thousands of miles away. Sick and injured people in remote areas of the world may have access to medical care—and even access to specialists—that they didn't have in the past.

## Amateur Communications Satellites

Amateur radio operators, called hams, are frequent users of communications satellites. In fact, they have their very own satellites, called hamsats. Since the 1970s, more than seventy satellites have been launched for the exclusive use of amateur radio operators. The majority of these satellites are the responsibility of the Radio Amateur Satellite Corporation (AMSAT), headquartered in Washington, D.C. It is an organization of volunteer spacecraft designers, builders, and operators from all over the world.

Hams became interested in space with the first *beep beep beep* of *Sputnik 1*. Later, they eagerly accepted the U.S. government's invitation to listen in on *Explorer 1*'s signals. It did not take long before the hams wanted their own satellite. The first was built by a group in California that called itself Project OSCAR (Orbital Satellite Carrying Amateur Radio). *OSCAR-1* was sent into space on December 12, 1961. It circled Earth for twenty-two days, beeping the Morse code signal for the letter *H* for "ham."

After the first four OSCAR satellites, AMSAT took over the series with *OSCAR-5*. By 2002 there were fifty OSCAR satellites. All of them have been designed, built, and financed by donations from hams in the United States, Germany, Canada, Great Britain, Australia, Russia, France, Italy, Japan, and many other nations. There have also been many non-AMSAT amateur communications satellites. The Radiosputnik series was launched by Russian hams, UoSATs by British hams, and the Fujis by Japanese hams.

Commercial satellites are usually launched by rockets owned by governments. Hams were originally able to send their little satellites into orbit for free. Governments allowed them to be included at no charge on rockets carrying commercial or scientific satellites. More recently, however, hams have had to pay fees for their hamsats to be launched.

The only problem facing communications satellites is their popularity and usefulness. There may simply be too many of them. There is only so much space available in geosynchronous orbit, and it is already getting overcrowded. Nearly one thousand communications satellites are providing services to civilians. Nearly eight hundred are used for military communications. One solution is to combine the functions of many satellites into a few large ones.

## Spies in the Sky

The military also found other applications for satellites. From the moment the balloon was invented in the eighteenth century, the military realized the value of being able to look from a great height upon an enemy. In fact, observers in balloons played an important role in the American Civil War (1861–1865). And when the airplane was invented, its first military application was observation. It is hardly surprising,

The Galactic Radiation and Background (GRAB) satellite was the United States' first intelligence—or "spy"—satellite. Launched in 1960, the satellite had a dual mission. The goal of the unclassified mission was to gather data on solar radiation. The secret mission involved detecting the radar pulses from Soviet equipment. Based on this information, analysts were able to determine that the Soviets had radar capable of detecting U.S. ballistic missiles.

then, that military advantages of satellites were not overlooked.

There are many ways in which satellites can be used to spy on an enemy. The use of cameras is the most obvious. A lot can be learned from photos taken from space, especially by observers specially trained to recognize important features. Pictures taken of a certain location over a period of time can be compared to see if any changes have occurred, for instance, and expert photo analysts can recognize missile installations or troop buildups.

High-resolution cameras using powerful telescopic lenses can obtain details as small as a license plate from an orbit 200 miles (322 km) above Earth. Spy satellites use many of the same methods employed by weather and Earth-monitoring satellites, such as heat sensors that can detect the infrared radiation emitted by factories and industries.

## War in Space

Satellites might take an even more active role in military operations. Even before the first satellites were launched, political and military leaders realized that satellites might be used as weapons in war. Originally, this idea was nothing more complicated than loading an orbiting satellite with bombs that could be dropped onto an enemy. Yet the development of the Intercontinental Ballistic Missile (ICBM) made this unnecessary.

The "ballistic" part of the missile's name means that it travels like a shell fired from a cannon. The curved path that the shell follows from gun to target is called a ballistic trajectory or ballistic path. A ballistic missile follows a similar curved path from the moment it takes off until it hits its target. Unlike a cannon, however, which might have a range of only a few hundred miles, the ballistic missile can hit a target thousands of miles away.

An ICBM can deliver a bomb much faster than a satellite, since a satellite could not drop its bombs until it was in the proper position—and that might take too long. Most modern research into satellite weapons involves equipping satellites with devices—such as lasers or small missiles—that could intercept and destroy ICBMs or enemy spy satellites.

This concept took a great leap forward in 1983. President Ronald Reagan announced his plans for a Strategic Defense Initiative (SDI). SDI would provide a kind of impenetrable shield over the United States, protecting the country from enemy attack. It would be accomplished by employing a wide array of space-based defense systems.

Some of these defense systems seemed straight out of science fiction. (In fact, the entire SDI program sounded so science fictional that most newspapers referred to it as "Star Wars.") For instance,

An artist's concept of a Space Laser Satellite Defense System developed during the 1980s as part of U.S. president Reagan's Strategic Defense Initiative

satellites would be equipped with rail guns that could shoot down enemy satellites and ICBMs. A rail gun would use projectiles accelerated by magnetic waves. The projectiles could be shot at such great speed that they would not even have to be explosive—they could be little more than lumps of metal or rock. The impact would be so great that it would have the same effect as an explosion.

There could also be particle beam weapons. These weapons would use beams of high-energy nuclear particles to disable enemy craft. Tests were made on the possibility of using lasers and X-rays as weapons. The latter would be powerful enough to disintegrate enemy missiles.

Although a great deal of research was carried out on these and other space-based weapons—some of it with great success—interest in the program waned. This was due in part to a lack of money to fund it and also to the collapse of the Soviet Union. Without its old enemy, the United States didn't seem to need such an expensive, complex defense shield any longer.

In modern times, most military satellites are used for communications and surveillance. Some of these satellites carry early warning systems that look for the telltale signs of missile launches or nuclear explosions. Others carry powerful telescopic cameras that can photograph objects on the ground as small as a few inches—just how much detail is possible is a closely guarded secret.

# 8 ORBITING OTHER WORLDS

From the time the first artificial satellites began orbiting Earth, scientists thought about the possibility of satellites orbiting other planets. Until they were able to do that, however, they had to be content with flyby missions to other worlds. Flybys occur when a spacecraft zooms past a planet, taking pictures and gathering as much information as it can during the few hours or minutes it is closest to its subject.

Such a mission costs millions of dollars and takes years to prepare. Plus, it takes months for a spacecraft to reach another planet. To the scientists, a handful of photos and a few minutes' worth of information didn't seem like enough payoff for all that effort. On the other hand, if a spacecraft could be placed into orbit around another world, then it could take photos and gather information for months and perhaps even years.

*Top:* This is an image from the Moon of a crater called Copernicus. The photo was taken in 1966 by the *Lunar Orbiter 2* satellite. *Middle:* An artist's depiction shows the space shuttle launching the *Galileo* spacecraft to Jupiter in 1989. *Bottom:* An artist's depiction shows *Cassini* in orbit around Saturn.

Yet, it is relatively simple to send a spacecraft past a planet. A successful flyby consists of nothing more than the spacecraft getting close to its target. Putting a spacecraft into orbit is much more complicated. Success requires that the satellite be launched into an exact orbit. It's like hitting a bull's-eye with a dart.

Putting a satellite into orbit 200 miles (322 km) above Earth is easy compared to placing one into orbit around a world millions of miles away. It is like comparing a sharpshooter hitting a target only a few feet away with a sharpshooter in New York trying to hit a target in Los Angeles. In order to achieve a stable orbit, a spacecraft has to arrive at precisely the right place at precisely the right time. If anything is even a little bit off, the spacecraft may simply shoot past the planet and disappear into space. Or it may crash headlong onto the surface of the planet. Either way, it would be an unfortunate loss of an expensive project.

## From Earth to the Moon

The first interplanetary space probes, launched in the late 1950s, were sent to the body closest to Earth: the Moon. The series of simple probes was called the Rangers. These probes weren't designed to orbit the Moon or to even fly past it. They were sent straight at their target, taking as many pictures as they could while plunging toward the surface at thousands of miles an hour. Only three of the seven Ranger probes sent to the Moon successfully returned images.

However, all five spacecraft in the Lunar Orbiter program were successful. Between August 1966 and August 1967, the Lunar Orbiters photographed 99.5 percent of the Moon's surface, including the far side (the side of the Moon that faces away from Earth) and south pole. Although it didn't do so intentionally, one of the Lunar Orbiters caught Earth hovering above the lunar horizon. This was the first photo ever taken of Earth as seen from the Moon. Another photo was a spectacular panorama of the crater Copernicus. It was hailed as "the photo of the century."

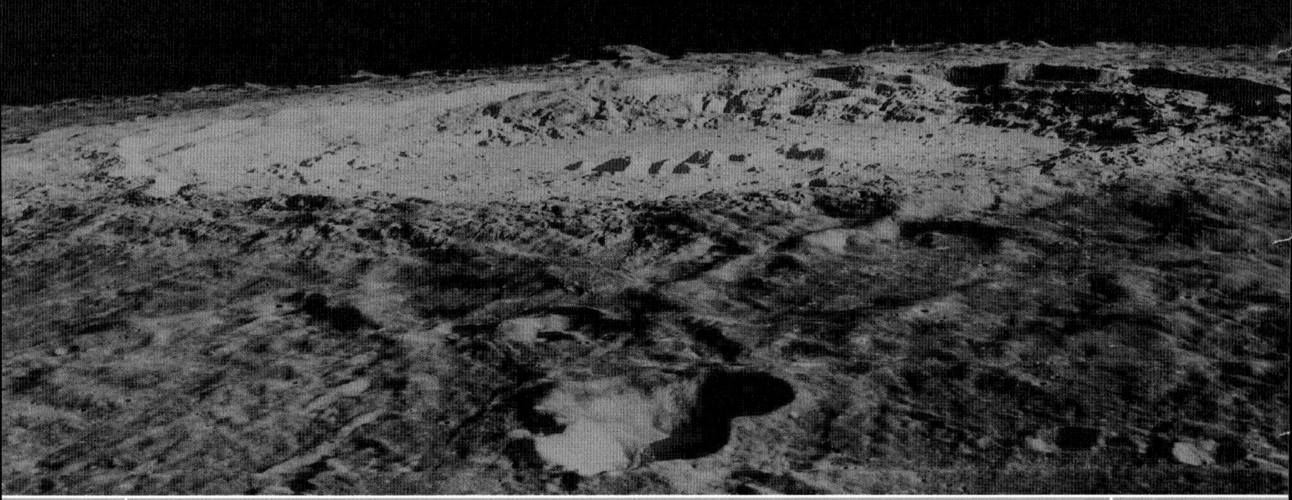

This spectacular view of the crater Copernicus, taken in 1966 by the *Lunar Orbiter 2* satellite, was called "the photo of the century."

The main objective of the Lunar Orbiters was to discover potential landing sites for the Apollo lunar landing program. But they also made many important scientific discoveries. For instance, variations in their orbits revealed the presence of huge concentrations of mass under the lunar "seas." These mass concentrations—called mascons for short—could be remnants of the huge asteroids whose impact created them. Twelve of these mass concentrations were discovered on the near side alone.

Five Lunar Orbiters circling the Moon in many different orbits would have caused complications for the astronauts who would soon be arriving. It would have been like trying to cross a busy street with traffic coming from every direction. Therefore, all of the Lunar Orbiters were deliberately crashed into the Moon when their missions were completed.

More than twenty years later, NASA planned to resume exploring the Moon with robots using their *Clementine* orbiter. NASA was able to implement a "faster, better, cheaper" approach to the construction of spacecraft and the planning of missions. *Clementine* moved from conceptual design to launch in only twenty-two months, and cost just $80 million. NASA saved money by using off-the-shelf technology—that is, technology that already existed—instead of specially designed instruments and equipment. It was the first time this approach had been used in a space program. The costs of previous deep space missions had been significantly higher and took a great deal more time to develop.

*Clementine* was launched on January 25, 1994. Officially known as the Deep Space Program Science Experiment (DSPSE), its main mission was the complex task of mapping the Moon. It succeeded beyond all expectations.

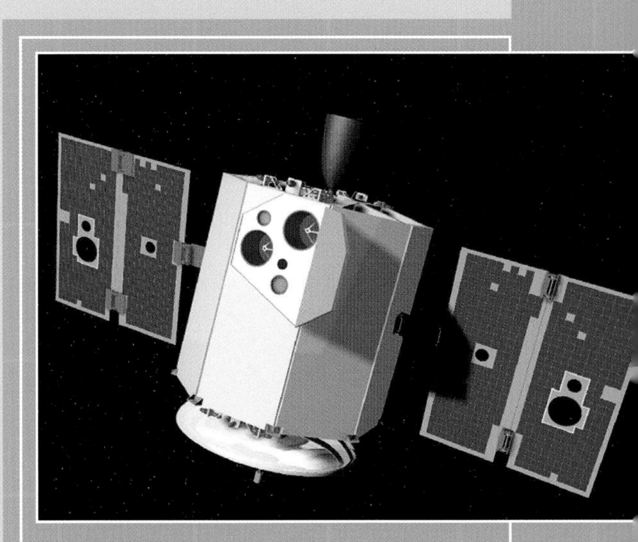

The *Clementine* satellite orbited the Moon, returning much data and many images, which allowed scientists to create the most highly detailed map of the Moon ever created. One of *Clementine*'s most spectacular discoveries was the possible presence of water ice near the lunar poles. Water on the Moon would be of great importance to the establishment of a human colony there.

Between February 26 and April 22, 1994, *Clementine* sent more than 1.8 million digital images of the Moon back to Earth. These images were quickly made accessible to the public via the Internet. The scientists examining the data from *Clementine* made a major scientific discovery. They saw the possible existence of ice within some of the Moon's craters, especially those located near its south pole, which are permanently shaded from the Sun's rays. This discovery was confirmed years later by another orbiter, NASA's *Lunar Prospector*.

In 1994 U.S. president Bill Clinton cited *Clementine* as one of the major national achievements in space exploration. "The relatively inexpensive, rapidly built spacecraft constituted a major revolution in spacecraft management and design," he said.

## Venus

The 1970s and 1980s were highlighted by the number of spacecraft sent by the United States and the Soviet Union to the planet Venus. Two U.S. spacecraft, *Pioneer-Venus 1* and *Pioneer-Venus 2*, reached their goal in 1978. The first orbited the planet, sending back data, while the second released probes that returned data from Venus's surface.

One of the first things discovered was how hot the surface of Venus is. At about 700°F (370°C), it is hot enough to melt lead! The greenhouse effect is responsible for the high temperatures. The greenhouse effect is caused by Venus's heavy atmosphere of carbon dioxide, which acts like a thermal blanket. It allows heat from the Sun to bake the surface of Venus but does not let heat escape back out into space.

Perhaps one of the most successful and important of all the satellites sent to Venus was the United States' *Magellan* orbiter, launched in 1989. It carried out a radar-mapping mission from 1989 to 1994 as it orbited Venus. Although Venus's dense clouds cannot be penetrated by visible light, other wavelengths, such as radar, can penetrate them. Maps are created by measuring the strength of the signal bouncing back from the surface. The maps reveal—in astonishing detail—the features on Venus's surface.

Using its radar, *Magellan* created the first ultrahigh resolution mapping of the planet's surface features. Scientists had been able to

The *Magellan* spacecraft is being prepared for launch to orbit the planet Venus. The enormous size of the satellite is revealed by the tiny figure of the technician (wearing white) at the lower left.

create globes of Venus based on the low-resolution radar images from prior Venus missions. These globes revealed general, continent-sized formations but very little detail. *Magellan*, however, finally allowed detailed imaging and analysis of craters, hills and mountains, ridges, plains, and other geologic formations. These images are comparable to the visible-light photographic mapping of other planets. *Magellan*'s

## Magellan's Launch

The *Magellan* orbiter was named after the sixteenth-century Portuguese explorer Ferdinand Magellan, whose expedition was the first to sail entirely around the world. It was the first interplanetary spacecraft to be launched by a space shuttle. The shuttle *Atlantis* carried *Magellan* into low Earth orbit, where it was released from the shuttle's cargo bay. A solid-fuel motor then fired, sending *Magellan* on a fifteen-month cruise into the inner solar system. After looping around the Sun one and a half times, the spacecraft finally arrived near Venus on August 10, 1990. A solid-fuel motor on *Magellan* then fired, placing the spacecraft in orbit around the planet.

By the end of its first 243-day cycle of orbits, *Magellan* had sent to Earth detailed images of 84 percent of Venus's surface. It did this twice more between 1991 and 1992, eventually creating detailed maps of 98 percent of Venus. Having duplicate maps, such as these, enabled scientists to detect any changes that might have occurred on the surface between cycles. *Magellan* also took images from slightly different angles, enabling scientists to reconstruct realistic three-dimensional views of the planet's surface.

global radar map will remain the most detailed map of Venus in existence for the foreseeable future. There are no plans for robotic missions to try to surpass its resolution.

### First Missions to Mars

In August and September 1975, the United States launched a pair of probes to Mars called *Viking 1* and *Viking 2*. They arrived nearly three weeks apart in July and August 1976. Both spacecraft consisted of two parts: an orbiter and a lander. For sixteen days, *Viking 1* circled the planet, surveying its surface for potential landing sites. A spot in a plain called Chryse Planitia was selected, and the lander was released. It touched down on July 20. *Viking 2* made its landing in Utopia Planitia several weeks later.

While the landers were analyzing the Martian soil and taking measurements on the surface, the two orbiters were busy mapping the surface. The more than forty thousand photos taken showed features as small as 33 feet (10 m). The photos allowed scientists to create the first detailed map of Mars. The orbiters and landers continued to transmit data for several more years, with the last transmission from *Viking 1* occurring in November 1982.

NASA's next mission to Mars was the *Mars Global Surveyor (MGS)*, in 1996. This mission was the first successful U.S. mission to the red planet in twenty years. It reached Mars on September 12, 1997. In March 1999, the spacecraft began its primary mission of mapping Mars.

The *Mars Global Surveyor* held a low-altitude polar orbit of 240 miles (386 km). This low orbit allowed the *MGS* to observe every region of the Martian surface during the planet's rotation. The *MGS*'s telescopic cameras allowed it to take images revealing details as small as 3 feet (1 m). Its Thermal Emission

The *Mars Global Surveyor* is being prepared by technicians at NASA's Jet Propulsion Laboratory in California for launch into orbit around Mars.

Spectrometer gathered data about the composition of the surface, ice, atmospheric dust, and clouds.

Perhaps most important, the Mars Orbiter Laser Altimeter (MOLA) on the *MGS* measured the height of surface features. MOLA did this by bouncing hundreds of millions of laser pulses from the Martian surface. It then measured the time it took for the light to make the round-trip. The quicker a pulse returned, the higher the terrain was (that is, the closer it was to the spacecraft). The longer it took, the lower the surface. Scientists were able to construct an accurate topographic map of Mars. A topographic map depicts the three-dimensional contours of a region.

The *MGS* has returned more data about the red planet than all other Mars missions combined. Among the most important discoveries made by *MGS* is the clear evidence that Mars once had an abundant supply of liquid water. *MGS* showed that a great deal of this water may still remain on the planet in the form of huge reservoirs of underground ice. Evidence for flowing water includes many different types of erosion features, such as channels, riverbeds, and gullies.

## Mars in the Twenty-First Century

NASA's *Mars Odyssey* arrived in orbit around Mars in 2001. Its mission was to study minerals, look for signs of water, and map the surface in more detail than ever before. Engineers had equipped the orbiter to look for water ice by detecting hydrogen in the atmosphere, since water contains hydrogen. Over centuries, small amounts of hydrogen leak from underground deposits of ice. One of the results of this search was the discovery of vast quantities of underground ice at both the north and south polar regions.

The most recent robotic mission to Mars is NASA's *Mars Reconnaissance Orbiter (MRO)*. Launched in August 2005, it arrived

## The European Space Agency

The European Space Agency (ESA) launched its first Mars mission in June 1993. Like the earlier Viking mission, the *Mars Express* spacecraft consisted of an orbiter and a lander. The lander was called *Beagle-2*. (It was named for the *Beagle*, the ship that carried Charles Darwin on his voyage of discovery.) However, *Beagle-2* was lost soon after its release from the orbiter. But the orbiter has worked perfectly and has returned invaluable information to Earth. It has revealed strong evidence for the presence of water ice on Mars. It also showed erosion features created by water flowing on the surface of ancient Mars. The orbiter has taken some of the most spectacular photos of Mars. Its High Resolution Stereo Color camera (HRSC) produces detailed, three-dimensional images of features as small as 6.5 feet (2 m).

in orbit around Mars in March 2006. Similar in many ways to the earlier *Mars Global Surveyor*, *MRO* carries the most powerful telescopic camera to ever scrutinize the surface of the red planet. It can obtain clear photographs of objects on the surface as small as 1 foot (0.3 m) from an altitude of 186 miles (300 km).

Among *MRO*'s other cameras is the Mars Color Imager. This is a wide-angle, low-resolution camera that views the surface of Mars in five visible and two ultraviolet bands of light. Each day it collects about eighty-four images, producing a detailed global map. The map will provide a daily weather report for Mars, help to determine its seasonal and annual variations, and map the presence of water vapor and ozone in its atmosphere. Other instruments will study Mars's gravity; send radar to penetrate the ice at the polar caps; and measure temperature, pressure, water vapor, and dust levels.

*MRO*'s mission lasted for two Earth years. One of the goals was to map the Martian landscape with high-resolution cameras in order to choose landing sites for future missions. These cameras can take

The *Mars Reconnaissance Orbiter (MRO)* is designed to search for water on Mars. Its instruments allow for extreme close-up photography of the Martian surface, the analysis of minerals, and a search for subsurface water. They also trace how much dust and water are distributed in the atmosphere and monitor daily global weather. This information will help scientists determine if there are deposits of minerals that form in water over long periods of time and if there is evidence for shorelines of ancient seas and lakes.

such detailed images that they have been able to discern the Viking lander on the surface.

## Jupiter

The *Galileo* probe to Jupiter was to have been launched by the space shuttle *Challenger*. However, when *Challenger* exploded only seventy-three seconds after takeoff on January 28, 1986, the *Galileo* project was put on hold until the cause of the accident was determined and corrections made to avoid future accidents. Finally launched in 1989 by the space shuttle *Atlantis*, *Galileo*'s prime mission was a two-year study of the Jupiter system.

After a journey of six years, *Galileo* went into orbit around Jupiter in 1995, with each orbit lasting about two months. The orbits were designed to allow the spacecraft to make close-up flybys of several of Jupiter's largest moons, including Io and Europa.

*Galileo* performed many scientific experiments, in addition to taking thousands of highly detailed photos. It discovered ammonia in Jupiter's atmosphere. This was the first time this important organic molecule had been observed in the atmosphere of another planet. *Galileo* closely observed volcanic activity on Io, revealing that it is a hundred times greater than that on Earth. *Galileo* also discovered that a powerful electrical current connects Io with Jupiter.

In 1994 *Galileo* was perfectly positioned to watch the fragments of Comet Shoemaker-Levy 9 crash into the night side of Jupiter. Terrestrial telescopes had to wait to see the enormous impact sites as they rotated into view. It was the first time a comet or asteroid had been observed hitting another planet. Scientists were anxious to see what the results of such a collision would be.

Perhaps the most exciting discovery *Galileo* made was strong evidence for a vast ocean of

These artist's depictions show the *Galileo* spacecraft, which was launched into orbit around Jupiter. The satellite and its booster were carried into orbit by the space shuttle, which is seen in the background of the top photo. Once *Galileo* was released from the cargo bay, its own engine boosted it toward the planet Jupiter *(above bottom)*, where it arrived six years later.

liquid water under the icy crust of Europa. Many scientists believe that this may be one of the best places to look for other life-forms in the solar system, since liquid water is vital to the existence of life as we know it.

*Galileo* ended its mission on September 21, 2003, after fourteen years in space and eight years in orbit around Jupiter. It was allowed to plunge into Jupiter's atmosphere, where it was vaporized. Scientists did this because they feared that if they left *Galileo* in orbit, it might one day crash into one of Jupiter's moons. A crash could contaminate a moon with organisms from Earth.

## SATURN

The Cassini-Huygens mission to Saturn was a joint mission developed by the European Space Agency and NASA. Launched in October 1987, it consisted of two spacecraft. *Cassini* went into orbit around the ringed planet, and *Huygens* made a soft landing on Saturn's giant moon, Titan.

Launched from Earth by a powerful U.S. Air Force Titan IVB/Centaur launch vehicle, *Cassini* arrived at Saturn on July 1, 2004, after a seven-year journey. The spacecraft flew through a gap in the thin outermost ring and entered orbit around Saturn. It was the first spacecraft ever to do so.

Only a day later, *Cassini* made its first distant flyby of Saturn's largest moon, Titan. It approached within 211,000 miles (339,000 km). Photographs were taken through filters able to see through the dense haze that covers the moon. They showed south polar clouds thought to be composed of methane and surface features with widely differing brightness. On closer passes, radar imagery revealed that much of the surface of Titan is relatively flat. Surface features are no more than 150 feet (50 m) high. During one of these passes, *Cassini* released the *Huygens* lander.

An artist's depiction of *Cassini* in orbit around Saturn

*Cassini* made flybys of the moon Enceladus, discovering that it has a thin atmosphere of water vapor. *Cassini* also observed enormous water ice geysers erupting from the south polar region. Scientists speculate that these geysers may be fueled by underground pockets of water. Enceladus may be one of the few bodies in our solar system with liquid water.

Since its arrival in orbit around Saturn, *Cassini* has returned a vast amount of new information about the planet. It has taken some of the most spectacular images ever of Saturn—or of any other planet, for that matter.

## Asteroids and Comets

The primary goal of the Near Earth Asteroid Rendezvous (NEAR) mission was to study the asteroid 433 Eros from orbit for approximately

The asteroid Eros was photographed up close by the NEAR spacecraft.

one year. Eros is the second-largest near-Earth asteroid. It has a cashew-shaped body about 8 x 8 x 20 miles (13 x 13 x 33 km) in size.

The NEAR spacecraft went into orbit in April 2000, eventually circling Eros at a distance of about 22 miles (35 km). It took hundreds of detailed close-up photos, as well as thousands of measurements of the asteroid's composition. The mission ended with the spacecraft touching down onto Eros's surface on February 12, 2001.

Since asteroids are ancient objects, they may give scientists clues to the origin of the solar system. Also, because there is a danger of an asteroid impacting Earth in the future, the more scientists can learn about them, the better they can plan ways to prevent such an occurrence.

The European Space Agency's *Rosetta* spacecraft was launched on March 2, 2004. A rendezvous with Comet 67P/Churyumov-Gerasimenko is planned in 2014. When *Rosetta* arrives, it will enter a slow orbit around the comet. *Rosetta* will then slow down gradually in preparation for releasing a lander that will touch down on the comet's surface.

The lander, named *Philae*, will approach the comet slowly. When it makes contact with the surface, *Philae* will fire two harpoons into the comet so the lander won't bounce off. Then it will attach itself to the comet with additional drills. *Philae* will begin a science mission that will determine the characteristics of the comet's nucleus, its chemical makeup, and how the comet behaves over time.

## Future Planetary Orbiters

Scientists have perfected many of the techniques for placing probes into orbit around other planets. They have also developed simpler, cheaper spacecraft. Because of these advances, scientists are planning missions to many other planets, their moons, and even other asteroids and comets.

Only one spacecraft has ever visited the planet Mercury. *Mariner 10* flew past the planet three times from 1974 to 1975. While it made some significant discoveries and returned hundreds of close-up photos, it was unable to examine the entire surface of the planet. Many questions and mysteries remain about the planet closest to the Sun. Scientists are eagerly looking forward to the *Mercury Messenger* orbiter. It will go into orbit around Mercury in 2011, allowing scientists to examine the planet in unprecedented detail.

One of the most exciting future missions is the spacecraft that is planned to orbit Jupiter's moon, Europa. The mission will focus on researching the possibility of a vast liquid ocean under the ice crust that covers the moon. The preliminary orbiter will use radar to penetrate the ice. This could reveal the water that may exist beneath.

Plans for the mission include hydrobots, which are tiny, robotic, submarine-like devices. They would melt their way through the ice and analyze the sea beneath. If an ocean exists, it would certainly be an interesting place, since everything that life needs to evolve could be found there: liquid water, warmth, and a rich mixture of chemicals. If a life-form exists in Europa's hidden ocean, scientists are eager to discover it.

# 9 THE FUTURE

Nearly every week of the year, new satellites are being launched into orbit: communications satellites, Earth observation satellites, weather satellites, and many more. Among the most important of these are the satellites that will help us better understand the planet we live on.

NASA's new CloudSat satellites are the first to study clouds on a global basis. Their data will contribute to better predictions of clouds and their role in climate change. Meanwhile, the *Hydros* satellite will give scientists global information about soil moisture and other data. This will help improve our understanding of how water, energy, and carbon are interchanged between Earth's land and atmosphere.

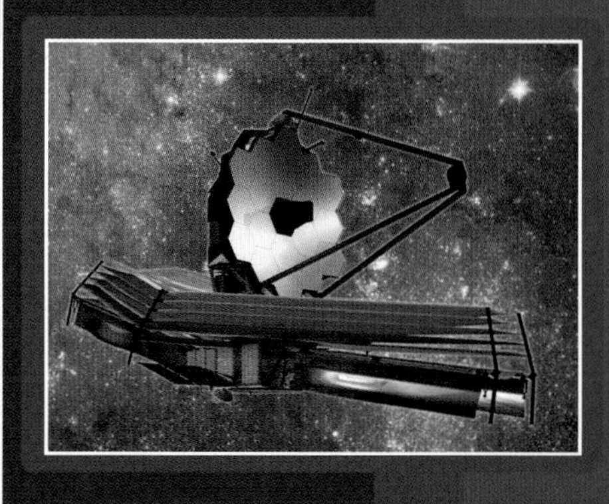

*Top: Dawn*, part of NASA's Discovery Program, will orbit Vesta and Ceres, two of the largest asteroids in the solar system. *Middle:* The James Webb Space Telescope (JWST) is scheduled for launch in 2013. JWST is expected to find the first galaxies that formed in the early universe and see stars forming planetary systems. *Bottom:* Space elevators could allow passengers and cargo to travel to and from space along a superstrong cable, just like elevators in tall buildings.

Other new satellites will provide global maps of salt concentrations in the oceans. This will help scientists understand how the oceans store and move heat. This is an important issue in the study of global warming, weather, and climate change.

Also, global warming causes polar ice and glaciers to melt and release freshwater into the oceans. Satellites will enable scientists to track these changes. This will not only affect the survival of many species but the fishing industry, as well. Satellites such as these will help us better understand how Earth works.

## Into the Future

Among the most exciting of the new satellites being planned are those meant to observe the universe around us. There are plans already in progress for the next generations of space telescopes. The James Webb Space Telescope will be an orbiting infrared observatory. It will orbit about 930,000 miles (1.5 million km) from Earth.

The Webb will be the replacement for the aging Hubble. It will have eighteen mirror segments that will unfold to form its primary mirror. This segmented mirror will be 21 feet (6.4 m) wide. This is more than two and a half times larger than Hubble's mirror. As large as this is, astronomers are already planning orbiting telescopes with mirrors up to 165 feet (50 m) wide. With telescopes such as these, astronomers hope to discover planets orbiting other stars and obtain pictures of them.

Another exciting future possibility is the space elevator. Scientists have been thinking about how a satellite in geostationary orbit seems to "hover" above a single spot on Earth's surface, like a helicopter hovering over its landing pad. If the helicopter can lower a rope to someone standing on the ground, why couldn't a cable connect a geosynchronous satellite to Earth?

If that could be done, then there could be direct communication between the ground and the satellite. This could include information, as well as physical objects. It could be a kind of "space elevator." If it were large enough, human beings could be carried into space and back again. This could be as simple and easy as traveling to the top of a tall building in an ordinary elevator.

The idea for the space elevator was first suggested many decades ago. But it was considered to be little more than an engineering fantasy—simply a mathematical possibility. No materials could withstand the enormous gravitational strains that would be involved. However, synthetic materials, such as carbon fibers, have been developed that possess incredible strength and other characteristics. The space elevator has been slowly coming off the drawing boards and is getting closer to reality.

A time may come—perhaps in the not-too-distant future—when traveling into space will not require specialized training. You will not have to strap yourself into an expensive, complex rocket. All you'll have to do is step into an elevator. When you step out of it a few minutes later, you'll be in a giant satellite orbiting Earth.

## GLOSSARY

**ablation:** the erosion of a heat protective surface material by aerodynamic friction, such as in a spacecraft's heat shield that is designed to wear away in order to prevent heat from building up in structurally important parts

**alchemist:** a practitioner of alchemy, a precursor of chemistry. One of the goals of alchemy was to discover a method for turning metals into gold.

**atmosphere:** the blanket of gases that surrounds a planet

**aurora:** the effect of electrically charged particles from the Sun striking the upper atmosphere of Earth

**black hole:** the result of a dying star collapsing upon itself. As it shrinks, its density and gravitational pull increase until a point is reached when even light itself cannot escape the surface.

**booster:** a rocket used to accelerate an object

**cosmic rays:** radiation of high penetrating power that originates in outer space. It consists partly of high energy atomic nuclei.

**density:** the amount of mass contained within a specific volume

**Geiger counter:** a device for detecting and measuring radioactivity. It was named for the German physicist Hans Geiger (1882–1945), who invented it with W. Müller.

**geosynchronous (geostationary):** an orbit at such a distance from Earth that a satellite placed there will seem to hover above one point on the planet

**launch vehicle:** a rocket used to accelerate an object into orbit, also sometimes called a "booster"

**light-year:** the distance light travels in one year, or about 5.8 trillion miles (9.5 trillion km)

**liquid fuel:** rocket fuel in the form of a liquid, such as gasoline, kerosene, or hydrogen

**magnetic field:** a region in which magnetic forces can be observed

**meteor:** the flash of light created when a meteoroid strikes Earth's atmosphere (sometimes called a "shooting star")

**meteoroid:** a small metallic or rocky body in space

**meteorologist:** a scientist who studies the weather and climate

**molecule:** a compound of two more atoms

**near space:** the region of outer space just beyond Earth's atmosphere

**nose cone:** the end of a rocket opposite its engine that contains the payload or cargo

**orbit:** the path a spacecraft follows as it circles a planet; the path a moon or planet follows as it circles a planet or the Sun

**organic molecule:** a molecule containing at least one carbon atom

**oxidizer:** a chemical that provides the oxygen necessary for the combustion of a fuel

**ozone:** a molecule of oxygen that consists of three atoms of oxygen. Normal atmospheric oxygen consists of only two atoms.

**payload:** cargo carried by a rocket, including weapons, instruments, or human beings

**satellite:** any small object orbiting a larger one. The Moon is a satellite of Earth.

**solar wind:** a stream of electrically charged particles flowing from the Sun

**solid fuel:** rocket fuel in solid form, which usually combines both fuel and oxidizer in one substance, such as gunpowder

**space station:** a manned satellite circling Earth or another planet

**ultraviolet radiation:** an energetic form of light beyond the visible spectrum

**Van Allen radiation belts:** doughnut-shaped regions of radioactive particles circling Earth. They are named for U.S. physicist James A. Van Allen (1914–2006), who first recognized them.

## Source Notes

23–24 N. A. Rynin, *Interplanetary Flight and Communication* (Jerusalem: Israel Program for Scientific Translations, 1971), 151.

79 Gary Federici, "Satellites for Strategic Defense," chap. 2 in *From the Sea to the Stars: A History of U.S. Navy Space and Space-Related Activities,* July 17, 2003, http://www.history.navy.mil/books/space/Chapter2.htm (April 23, 2007).

87 James R. Hansen, "To Behold the Moon: The Lunar Orbiter Project," chap. 10 in *Spaceflight Revolution,* 1994, http://history.nasa.gov/SP-4308/ch10.htm (April 23, 2007).

88 Howard McCurdy, *Faster, Better, Cheaper: Low Cost Innovation in the U.S. Space Program* (Baltimore: Johns Hopkins University Press, 2001), 117.

90 U.S. Naval Research Laboratory, "The Clementine Mission," *Center for Computational Science,* July, 13, 2006, http://www.cmf.nrl.navy.mil/clementine (April 23, 2007).

## Selected Bibliography

Gatland, Kenneth. *The Illustrated Encyclopedia of Space Technology*. London: Orion Books, 1989.

Ley, Willy. *Rockets, Missiles, and Men in Space*. New York: Signet, 1968.

Ordway, Frederick I., and Wernher von Braun. *The Rockets' Red Glare*. Nelson, NZ: Anchor Press, 1976.

——. *Space Travel: A History*. New York: Harper & Row, 1985.

## For Further Information

### Books

Burrows, William E. *This New Ocean: The Story of the First Space Age*. New York: Random House, 1998.

Clary, David A. *Rocket Man: Robert H. Goddard and the Birth of the Space Age*. New York: Theia Books, 2004.

Cobb, Allan B. *Weather Observation Satellites*. New York: Rosen, 2003.

Crouch, Tom D. *Aiming for the Stars: The Dreamers and Doers of the Space Age*. Washington, DC: Smithsonian Institution Scholarly Press, 2000.

Elish, Dan. *Satellites*. Salt Lake City: Benchmark Books, 2006.

Gaffney, Timothy R. *Secret Spy Satellites: America's Eyes in Space*. Berkeley Heights, NJ: Enslow, 2000.

Johnson, Rebecca L. *Satellites*. Minneapolis: Lerner Publications Company, 2005.

Kupperberg, Paul. *Spy Satellites*. New York: Rosen, 2003.

Miller, Ron. *Rockets*. Minneapolis: Twenty-First Century Books, 2008.

Sherman, Josepha. *Deep Space Observation Satellites*. New York: Rosen, 2003.

Spangenburg, Ray, and Kit Moser. *Artificial Satellites*. Danbury, CT: Frankin Watts, 2000.

Ward, Bob. *Dr. Space: The Life of Wernher von Braun*. Annapolis, MD: Naval Institute Press, 2005.

**Magazines**

*Ad Astra*
http://www.nss.org/
This is the official magazine of the National Space Society.

*Quest*
http://www.spacebusiness.com/quest/
This magazine is devoted to space history.

**Museums**

Kansas Cosmosphere and Space Center
1100 N. Plum
Hutchinson, KS 67501
http://www.cosmo.org/visitorinfo/whyhutch.php

Kennedy Space Center
State Road 405
Kennedy Space Center, FL 32899
http://www.kennedyspacecenter.com

Pima Air & Space Museum
6000 E. Valencia Rd.
Tucson, AZ 85706
http://www.pimaair.org/

San Diego Air & Space Museum
2001 Pan American Plaza
Balboa Park, San Diego, CA 92101
http://www.aerospacemuseum.org/

Smithsonian National Air & Space Museum
6th & Independence SW
Washington, DC 20560
http://www.nasm.si.edu/

U.S. Space and Rocket Center
One Tranquility Base
Huntsville, AL 35805
http://www.spacecamp.com/museum/

**Websites**

Encyclopedia Astronautica
http://www.friends partners.org/mwade/spaceflt.htm
This website provides an online encyclopedia of spacecraft and space history.

NASA History Office Home Page
http://www.hq.nasa.gov/office/pao/History/history.html
This website shows NASA's recent and upcoming events, NASA's publications, NASA documents, and more.

NASA Home Page
http://www.nasa.gov/
The official website of the National Aeronautics and Space Administration provides current mission photos and news.

Space.com Home Page
http://www.space.com/
This website provides daily news about happenings in space and astronomy.

Space Telescope Science Institute
http://www.stsci.edu/
This is the official website for the Hubble Space Telescope.

Students for the Exploration and Development of Space
http://www.seds.org
This student-based organization promotes the exploration and development of space with programs, publications, membership, and discussion forums.

# INDEX

## About the Author

Ron Miller is the author and illustrator of many books, most of which have been about science, space, and astronomy. His award-winning books include *The Grand Tour* and *The History of Earth*. Among his nonfiction books for young people are *Special Effects, The Elements*, and the Worlds Beyond series, which received the 2003 American Institute of Physics Award in Physics and Astronomy. His book *The Art of Chesley Bonestell* won the 2002 Hugo Award for Best Non-Fiction. He has also designed space-themed postage stamps and has worked as an illustrator on several science-fiction movies, such as *Dune* and *Total Recall*.



## Photo Acknowledgments

All images were provided by the author except p. 72 (AP Photo/Ron Kuenstler).

Cover: NASA